The Making of Sages

THE MAKING OF
SAGES

————— •◆• —————

Biblical Wisdom and
Contemporary Culture

————— •◆• —————

Donn F. Morgan

TRINITY PRESS INTERNATIONAL
Harrisburg, Pennsylvania

Trinity Press International, P.O. Box 1321, Harrisburg, PA 17105
Trinity Press International is a division of The Morehouse Group.

COVER ART: *Initial S with King David as Scribe*, Master of the Cypresses, Rosenwald Collection. Photograph © 2001 Board of Trustees, National Gallery of Art, Washington, D.C.
COVER DESIGN: Brenda Klinger

Library of Congress Cataloging-in-Publication Data
Morgan, Donn. F.
    The making of sages : biblical wisdom and contemporary culture / Donn F. Morgan.
       p. cm.
    Includes bibliographical references and index.
    ISBN 1-56338-328-4 (alk. paper)
    1. Wisdom literature—Criticism, interpretation, etc. 2. Wisdom—Biblical teaching. 3. Church and education. 4. Wisdom—Religious aspects—Christianity. I. Title.

BS1455 .M67 2002
223'.06—dc21   2001052458

Printed in the United States of America

02 03 04 05 06 07   10 9 8 7 6 5 4 3 2 1

Contents

Preface   vii

Acknowledgments   xi

Abbreviations   xiii

Introduction: Biblical and Contemporary Wisdom
in Dialogue: Who and Where Are the Sages?   xv

I. Understanding Biblical Sages

1. From Wisdom to Torah: The Pedagogy of the Sages   3

2. Confucius, Solomon, and Their Literature:
   The Making of Sages   15

3. Educational Roles and Pedagogical Methods:
   Teaching Wisdom and Creation in Proverbs   29

4. Behavioral Goals and Political Issues: The Sages and Hope   46

II. Locating Contemporary Sages

5. Sages and the University: Is There Wisdom in
   Higher Education?   57

6. Religious Educators: Professionals or Sages?   69

7. Biblical Sages and Modern Professionals:
   Strange Bedfellows or Variations on a Theme?   84

8. Leadership and Wisdom in a Time of Chaos:
   A Tale of Two Solomons   102

III. Identifying Biblical and Contemporary Sages: Education and Wisdom in Religious Communities

9. Education and the Church: A Biblical Perspective   113

10. The Sages and Contemporary Education in the Church   125

11. New Paradigms and Methods: Teaching the Wisdom
    of Israel in a New Land   138

12. Searching for Wisdom: Recent Biblical Studies and
    Their Pertinence for Contemporary Ministry   147

Conclusion: Searching for Sages in America:
Can the Bible Help?   160

Select Bibliography   171

Index   175

Preface

Who are the sages? How do we teach wisdom? And how are the answers to both of these questions related to the ongoing life of communities of faith who struggle with the discernment of wisdom in this world and with the never-ending challenges of education? I have posed these questions to many people. This book is the product of many different attempts to share some of what I have learned from others along the way, to deal with these questions and some of the answers. The diversity of essays in this volume is a testimony to their different origins and intentions. Indeed, the idea of collecting all the essays contained in this book was fairly recent.

Though I didn't know it at the time, this project began about fifteen years ago when my teaching of the Old Testament and research interests in biblical wisdom and canonical studies took an unexpected turn when I became an academic dean. Barbara Brown Zikmund, a colleague in administration, introduced me to the thought of Donald Schon and other educational theorists. My own previously modest interests in theological education expanded to include examining debates about the professions, exploring new technologies and pedagogies, and analyzing the overall character and shape of several types of educational institutions. As I tried to relate these new interests to my ongoing research in biblical wisdom literature, I gradually came to a realization that provides the rationale for this volume. If biblical wisdom and the sages are to be seen as pertinent and important today, some intentional relating of them to contemporary education and contemporary sages, or those who might have some functional parallels, needs to occur. Many of the chapters in this volume were born out of this conviction and of my attempts to begin such a dialogue between the biblical and modern.

Throughout this period I was also involved in the study of scripture from a particular canonical perspective. For me this has always meant understanding the Bible as one component in a dialogue between old and new, which characterizes every community with a scriptural canon. The value of wisdom literature in the canon has been subject to debate. It took me in directions and into dialogues I had never envisioned, some of which have found their way into this volume.

Readers of this study may go quickly to sections of special interest, for each of these chapters has its origin in a distinct setting. Others may wish to read the book as a whole, seeing it as I have—a journey with biblical wisdom and contemporary culture that attempts to deal with difficult but critical questions facing our faith communities and society at large. Most of the detail in these chapters pertains either to biblical wisdom and the sages who produced it, or to contemporary educational theory. I leave specific study of other cultures, religions, and the many manifestations of nonbiblical wisdom in the present day to those with more experience and expertise. What I hope for all, and commend to all, is that the old, biblical and classical, continue to be mixed with the new. This not only reflects a valuable and appropriate dynamic for all scriptural communities of faith; it also forces each of us to be open to the new, to the changing, to what the biblical sages would see as the mystery and the wonder of God.

A book that has taken this long to put together requires a great deal of thanks, for I have been encouraged and sustained by many over the years. I am much in debt to my colleagues in Old Testament scholarship, especially those who have studied sages and wisdom so long and so well. For the good people of Christ Church Cathedral in Indianapolis for inviting me to give a series of lectures on the Bible and education, I am grateful. The faculty and students of Chung Chi College at Chinese University in Hong Kong twice provided gracious hospitality and a wonderful setting for research in the 1990s. Many friends, supporters, and students of the Church Divinity School of the Pacific in Berkeley have given me insight, challenged my thoughts, and been extraordinarily patient as they heard me ask questions about sages and wisdom innumerable times, yet every time they helped me to learn more. For my wife, Alda Marsh Morgan, whose care about what I care about and whose support in quiet and unquiet ways was always there, "Thank you" is inadequate. Hal Rast of Trinity Press International first encouraged me to pursue bringing all of this material together, and his successor, Henry Carrigan, has enthusiastically, competently, and patiently continued the good oversight of this project. To both of these editor-scholar-publishers, and their great staff, I owe many thanks.

Most of all, however, I am aware that such a long-term project cannot be sustained by individual effort but needs to be nurtured in a context that encourages hard work and important research while still understanding the many other responsibilities that threaten to derail the best of plans. The faculty of my school, the Church Divinity School of the Pacific, have provided such a context for me and for many others. Because of them, with their commitment both to the best of scholarship and to faithful service to the Church, I had the ability and commitment necessary to finish this work. To these friends and colleagues, fellow searchers for wisdom, the faculty of the Church Divinity School of the Pacific, I dedicate this book.

Donn F. Morgan
22 March 2001

Acknowledgments

The following are reprinted with permission:

Donn F. Morgan. "Religious Educators: Professionals or Sages?" *Hong Kong Journal of Religious Education* 5 (December 1993): 15–28.

Donn F. Morgan. "Searching for Biblical Wisdom: Recent Studies and Their Pertinence for Contemporary Ministry." *Sewanee Theological Review* 37, no. 2 (Easter 1994): 151–62.

Abbreviations

BZAW	Beihefte zur Zeitschrift für die alttestamentliche Wissenschaft
HUCA	*Hebrew Union College Annual*
JBL	*Journal of Biblical Literature*
JSOTSup	Journal for the Study of the Old Testament: Supplement Series
KJV	King James Version
NRSV	New Revised Standard Version
OBO	Orbis biblicus et orientalis
RSV	Revised Standard Version
SBL	Society of Biblical Literature

Introduction
Biblical and Contemporary Wisdom in Dialogue: Who and Where Are the Sages?

Who are the sages? Where might we find them? These are difficult questions to answer. Are we asking ourselves a contemporary question or are we probing ancient sources for historical paradigms? Everyone searches for what the sages supposedly possess, namely, wisdom. If the sages do not have wisdom, they surely know the way to it. Perhaps, at least with regard to contemporary sages, it is not quite fair to say we are unable to identify them; rather, there is little or no consensus about how we can identify these wise people. Indeed, there is often great disagreement, for one person's sage is often another person's fool.

The following scenario aptly describes a search for wisdom, whether in the biblical period or the modern day. Someone, usually in relationship to a particular community with a set of common values (to live well, to be wise, to be rich and successful, to be slim and strong, or some variation on one or more of these themes), searches for wisdom and finds it. At least he thinks he has. And this wisdom is more often than not a combination of old and new, of things tried in times past and of new insights especially pertinent to the present day.[1] If the wisdom found actually allows the community to live well and

---

1. An interesting example of this phenomenon is found in the words of a famous chef, Marc Veyrat: "My cuisine is creative. . . . But I am also traditional. To create, you need a tradition on which to build" (*New York Times,* 14 March 2001, B1).

according to its stated values and purpose of life, then the searcher is often considered a sage. Consider the number of best-sellers that promise good and successful living (e.g. wealth, spiritual growth, loss of weight), with the resultant wealth and status of the wise author, which is itself often seen as an affirmation of his or her wisdom. But the innumerable popular proverbial writings, which sometimes do not bring wealth or status—indeed their writers are usually unknown—fulfill the same function for a community. In any case, regardless of the type of wisdom found and circulated, it often becomes frozen, fixed, in oral or literary forms that have scriptural or authoritative functions. Usually there are subsequent carriers and transmitters of this wisdom, sometimes having more status and authority than the original sage. These carriers of past wisdom are critically important, for they provide the way for interaction to occur between ever-changing circumstances and the formulations of the original sage, often written in a different time and place. Here then is a special challenge for those who would adhere to and learn from the wisdom of the past: Is there a means by which past wisdom can be rejuvenated, kept up-to-date, so that it will continue to accomplish its original purposes?

This problem or challenge is especially important when biblical wisdom is studied, for the sages of old are largely anonymous and gone from the contemporary scene. Indeed, we know precious little about the biblical sages as a group in ancient Israel. What we do know, or suppose, is that they were interested in more than finding wisdom; they also wanted to pass it on to their communities. We suppose further that the process by which they did this was not by publishing a best-seller or by utilizing any other means of widespread distribution but rather by teaching—to their families, to their students in a school setting, to leaders in the state or religious establishment. But how these wise ones taught is also very much of a mystery, creating the second major challenge with which this study deals.

There have been many significant attempts to study the sages of ancient Israel, their wisdom, and the ways they taught. The students of these sages have been primarily biblical scholars, though some religious educators also have explored these issues. We can enhance our knowledge of both biblical and modern sages by creating a dialogue. This dialogue must take seriously the paucity of knowledge we possess about biblical sages and the danger any body of wisdom has to become fixed, sterile, and ineffectual by failing to take into account the new, which calls for adaptation and reapplication of the old. Though there are many different dialogue partners possible, surely the biblical sages must be one. And, for the purposes of this study, I have chosen to see contemporary educational theorists, professionals, and communities of faith, primarily the Church, as dialogue partners with biblical sages. Surely there are other possibilities for dialogue partners, and from time to time I will refer to them. That more can and should be done in the future is clear. But a dialogue between ancient wisdom and contemporary communities, with a special focus on how such wisdom is transmitted and taught, will always be important in discussing the identity of the sages.

The individual chapters in this volume represent a series of forays into uncharted waters where the dialogue between wisdom and contemporary culture, between ancient and modern sages, occurs. There is no one method or particular approach represented by all of these chapters; rather, they reflect a few of the many different ways in which comparisons may be made. Some chapters are intentionally cross-disciplinary, for the search for wisdom requires immersion in areas of expertise and knowledge different from the biblical sages. In at least two chapters there are cross-cultural explorations, and here the comparative method is especially valuable and pertinent. There is, of course, a focus on things exegetical and historical, for these are disciplines and perspectives central to biblical scholarship. Finally, many of these chapters, perhaps especially the first, and all of those in the last section, intentionally look at confessional issues and the nature of wisdom. Since wisdom and sages are often in the eye of the beholder, subject to a particular community's perspective and judgment, the implications of these confessional issues must be faced head on; otherwise dialogue will be difficult, if not impossible.

Despite a somewhat eclectic series of methods in the individual chapters, there are two important perspectives central to understanding and coming to grips with the nature of the dialogue between sages and wisdom in ancient and modern times. These two perspectives are related directly to the challenges identified above: (1) the means by which wisdom is communicated or taught, and (2) the need for communities to relate wisdom of the past to new challenges and changing circumstances. There is also a focus on education. Sometimes this is a historical interest, exploring the nature of education in times past. Often contemporary educational theory adds a perspective that may help us to understand the ancient sages and how they might have taught their wisdom. Sometimes there is a more immediate concern, dealing with the problems and challenges of education in our own times. Then the perspectives of biblical wisdom are juxtaposed to our present educational issues in the hopes of providing insight and direction. Behind all of this lies a belief that the sages were and are carriers, transmitters, and conservators of wisdom and that teaching and communication were very important for the fulfilling of this function.

Many chapters in this volume interpret biblical material from a canonical perspective, that is, one that takes seriously the fact that this material is scripture. Such a perspective is important for at least two reasons. First, from a historical perspective, wisdom literature and the rise in importance of the sage took place in the postexilic period, when the nature of Judaism as a scriptural religion was firmly set. Second, a canonical approach also asks questions of the interrelationship between the different parts of scripture. Such questions provide valuable insights for understanding how ancient and modern wisdom relate to literature (and the functionaries usually associated with such literature, namely, priests and prophets), with different perspectives on revelation and authority.

The methods and perspectives found in these studies are diverse and eclectic, and they reflect only the tip of the iceberg of possibilities for this kind of study. I hope, however, that the educational issues and interests of the sages as well as the scriptural nature of ancient wisdom are seen as important for an ongoing dialogue between biblical wisdom and contemporary culture. I also hope that the dialogue begun here will be enriched with different perspectives and methods of others who search for wisdom.

Sages and Wisdom: Starting Points

Though perhaps this is the appropriate place to give a working definition of wisdom and the sage, it is perhaps best to avoid giving precise definitions, except to recognize that being wise and attaining wisdom have to do with living well. Put another way, assuming the purpose of life to be positive, wisdom will help one attain that purpose. The relationship between sages and wisdom is critically important, for the sages are primary vehicles for the production and communication of wisdom. Wisdom, however it is to be defined, is best understood by looking at those we call wise. By studying the institutions, roles, and literature with which sages are associated, and by examining their pedagogical methods and goals, we will better understand wisdom, both ancient and modern, and better be able to put these two expressions of how to live well into dialogue with one another.

The following theses, and their explanations, set forth the perspective about wisdom and sages found in this study.

1. *Wisdom and sages are referential terms, needing both a community and an object to be communicated in order to function properly.* Can wisdom exist by itself? Can sages exist by themselves? The answer to both these questions would appear to be no, for both terms presuppose relationships: wisdom to a community that considers it such, and sages to a body of wisdom they either produce, transmit, or conserve. In the biblical witness, one could argue that wisdom exists as an entity outside the community, dependent upon God. But even so, a community is needed to affirm that fundamental truth.

There are many implications in this thesis. Wisdom is not to be equated with the institution that orders or establishes the primary values of a society or culture, nor is the sage the primary authority figure (though the sage's function can be found in primary authority figures, such as Solomon or Jesus). Rather, wisdom and sages are used by institutions (e.g., the family, the monarchy, and the cultic establishment) to affirm the values and goals associated with them. Wisdom does not exist for itself. Sages do not exist for themselves.

2. *The social locus of a sage and the wisdom associated with that figure are dependent upon the way in which the community identifies and maintains its primary values, most often located in or near the institution most centrally associated with these values.* In ancient Israel, sages and other carriers of wisdom were associated with the monarchy, with the family, with schools. The figures of king and advisor, elder (of tribe and nuclear family), and teacher were most often assumed to be the ones who performed the functions of the sage or wise person. Consider the identity of the wise person in ancient Israel. With the exception of Solomon, we have only the wise men of Hezekiah (Proverbs), a few references to special individuals, and some oblique citations mentioning the wise as a class. There is no serious biblical discussion of what a sage did, where one could be found, or who the wise were, until the Wisdom of Jesus ben Sira. Because of this, most of our assumptions about sages are dependent upon the wisdom we associate with them and the institutions we believe valued such wisdom.

At one level, then, we may speak of sages as created by the culture—by a human community, which has particular values—and by wisdom, which affirms those values and their application to and for living well. To the extent that we have a cult-centered or a monarch-centered community and culture, it may be appropriate to speak of sages being created by the cult or monarchy and located in those places central to their values. When the values and major institutions of a society change, as was certainly the case in ancient Israel, to say nothing of the contemporary period, what the sage looks like and where the sage will be found will also change. While the story or mythos of the society may not change, it is the social institutions associated with that story and its values that determine who will be the sages and where we will find them. The more diverse the society and culture, the more sages and wisdom there are, though often with little or no consensus among groups competing for power and influence. How much a central story, with foundational values, can be embraced by all is not only determinative of whether we have pluralism instead of chaos or anarchy. It also determines whether sages will be speakers for values associated with the culture as a whole or are merely panhandlers of a particular way of viewing life, with little affirmation by the state, society, or culture.

3. *The social locus of sages most often testifies to the conservative nature of both them and the wisdom with which they are associated.* Not only are sages usually associated with particular institutions—indeed, they are actually created by them at one level—but sages are engaged in activities that promote the well-being and continuance of the institution, sometimes producing, sometimes teaching wisdom that rests upon institutional self-interest. Surely the sages can and do witness to dimensions of social and ideological reality that transcend the institutional forms in which such reality is made manifest. But the sage is rarely a vehicle for challenging the existence of such institutions, though corrective observations, usually dependent upon older (forgotten or neglected?) values, are certainly heard from sages from time to time. In biblical times, sages were rarely speakers for the new and potentially disruptive; they rarely were agents of change. Is this true in contemporary society as well?

Given the difficulty in biblical and contemporary times of defining and identifying sages with precision, we sometimes focus first on institutions where central values of societies are proclaimed and lived out. Here we might expect to find sages and their wisdom. But another approach found in some of the following chapters focuses on particular functions, roles, and institutions associated with them: teaching, analysis, proclamation of primary societal values. Since what is wise is often subject to much debate in contemporary society, the biblical material is brought as a gauge, providing a comparative dimension as well as a potentially normative perspective from which to evaluate who and what we consider wise today. Sages and the wisdom they teach and conserve are inextricably tied together. We know who sages are by the wisdom they are associated with. But the wisdom of the sage needs affirmation and acknowledgment from institutions and communities within society, making both sages and their wisdom derivative in nature.

Despite the difficulty in defining biblical wisdom and in determining exactly who sages were and what their roles in society were, the past generation of biblical scholarship has devoted a good deal of attention to wisdom literature and to the sages. Most of this scholarship has focused on the nature of biblical wisdom, with some special attention also given to the relationship of this peculiar literature to the more mainstream materials found in Torah and the Prophets. That the wisdom writings differ in both form and content from other biblical literature cannot be denied or easily dismissed. But there are also some fundamental common points (e.g., a retributional theological system, a heavy focus on morality, the figure of Wisdom seen as a prophetess, royal authority). The overall result of this new focus on wisdom literature has been an increased appreciation of its particular message and perspective. At the same time, scholars recognize that there are a number of important ways to integrate wisdom and the circle responsible for its creation, teaching, and transmission into the rest of the biblical message. This is in sharp contrast with the reigning opinion a generation ago of a tradition that was irrelevant, if not antithetical, to the primary messages of the Hebrew Bible. Such new ways of viewing wisdom, focusing on integration rather than separation, have searched for ways to relate the work and role of the shadowy figures of the sages to the major institutions of their day.

The present study is indebted to and rests upon this rich scholarship of the past that is devoted to biblical wisdom and sages. Yet I want to go a step further in attempting to see the importance of the sage for ancient Israel and today. Even with the increased attention to sages, their roles and functions remain blurry. The establishment of a dialogue between ancient and modern wisdom uses contemporary methods to understand ancient pedagogy. It also uses ancient values and stories to help understand the nature of contemporary professions that might well have functions and roles parallel to ancient sages. Such a dialogue, wherever it goes and whatever insights it gains, may help us better understand both ancient wisdom and the wisdom of our own day. Eclectic and wide-ranging though the dialogue begun by these chapters is, it is also reflective of the need for even more diversity and imagination as we seek to understand both old and new wisdom. We

must be ready to hear both affirmation of common values and disso-
nance, which will call us to careful reflection and decision making
about who and what is wise in our own times.

This study begins with a series of chapters focusing on the Bible.
There is a certain logic, perhaps even a normative priority, in such a
starting point. We begin searching for wisdom by looking at the biblical texts, specifically those texts that speak of wisdom explicitly.
Upon identifying such texts, we seek to learn more of the wisdom they
contain through some relatively traditional methods of exegesis. Once
we have understood the biblical message on its own terms, paying
attention to historical issues as they are important and determinable
(not always easy for wisdom literature), then we are ready to deal
with applying the meaning and message to contemporary society.

While there is logic to this type of approach, it does not reflect the
process of interpretation that is actually occurring. The fact is that we
do not begin our process of interpretation with the Bible. Rather, we
always begin, consciously or not, with contemporary concerns or values. Take, for example, the first chapter in this book: "Confessional
and Historical Issues: From Wisdom to Torah." This is ostensibly a historical study of the sages, tracing the development from biblical to
rabbinic to talmudic sages, with textual references and exegesis as
necessary and appropriate. At one level, we start with the appropriate texts and draw our conclusions on the basis of careful study. But,
very quickly, it becomes obvious that our view of sages and the religious values associated with them are dependent upon a number of
factors stemming from our faith commitments today. Perhaps more
importantly, our reasons for going to the sages of history come from
our contemporary need for sages today, for a tradition that holds on
to such teaching and the figures responsible for it. Thus, the dialogue
between the Bible and contemporary community—in our specific
case, between the wisdom of old and new—begins because we today
want and need it to occur. The Bible and the ancients who produced
it are incapable of starting the dialogue, though if we start it, they will
chime in with their perspectives to enrich us.

Organizational Rationale

The hope of this study is that the dialogue begun between ancient wisdom and contemporary culture, with special focus on the sages, their
roles and functions, will encourage others to continue the process.

While there is a rationale behind the present volume's organization, it is also true that each of the original essays or lectures were intended for separate occasions. How then should this book be read? The introduction and conclusion are intended to provide some perspective on the task at hand and the task still to be done. The individual chapters are best read sequentially, though if there are special interests that lead to an nonsequential reading, that would be in keeping with the genesis of the project itself.

The three major sections of this study represent different but related ways of dealing with the identity, roles, and functions of biblical and modern sages. Overall, this study wishes to (1) understand the nature, functions, and message of the sage; (2) locate places where sages might function and roles that sages might assume; and (3) explore the ways in which biblical sages might help the Church address contemporary challenges, especially in the area of education.

Section I (chapters 1–4) answers the question of what the sage is. Chapter 1 approaches this question from historical, confessional, developmental, and educational perspectives, focusing on the postexilic and rabbinic periods. Chapter 2 explores the making of sages with a comparative study of Solomon and Confucius and their wisdom canons. Chapter 3 focuses on the sage as teacher, comparing biblical wisdom literature with contemporary educational theory. Chapter 4 studies the concept of hope in biblical wisdom literature, drawing contemporary parallels and applications.

Section II (chapters 5–8) is concerned with determining where the sage might be found and what roles might be associated with this figure in both biblical and contemporary times. Chapter 5 focuses on the modern university, asking how this institution of learning can be related to the activities of ancient wisdom, both biblical and classical. Chapter 6 looks at the role of teaching from a dual perspective, namely, the histories of professionalization and education. Originally written in response to issues of contemporary significance in Hong Kong, this chapter raises issues concerning teachers and sages in a wide variety of contexts. Chapter 7 examines the role of the professional, comparing and contrasting it with that of the biblical sage and trying to shed light on both ancient and modern figures. Chapter 8 places contemporary leadership theory into dialogue with biblical wisdom and attempts to demonstrate both significant parallels and disparities between sages and modern leaders.

Section III (chapters 9–12) asks how the contemporary faith community might best use biblical wisdom literature in addressing the needs of education in both Church and society. Chapters 9, 10, and 11 were originally written together and represent a sequential approach to this concern. Chapter 9 describes the problem of education in the Church and a rationale for using biblical wisdom to address this problem. Chapter 10 explores the nature of the biblical sage and potential opportunities and challenges for the appropriation of this figure in the modern Church. Chapter 11 revisits the issue of pedagogy raised in chapter 3, focusing on particular ways in which the sage and teaching can be addressed in the Church. Chapter 12 provides both a history of the study of wisdom literature and the sages over the past thirty years and a representative bibliography that can be a starting point for future study and dialogue.

This book affirms that we have much to learn from sages, both ancient and modern. Indeed, it is much to our advantage to continue to seek them out and to identify them. A central thesis of this book, if also an irony, is that we are best able to understand sages of the biblical period and in our contemporary times by putting them into dialogue with one another. That is, we can learn more about ancient sages by relating them to contemporary wisdom, and we will learn more of what is wise and who are the carriers of wisdom today by relating the present day's search for wisdom to the ancient biblical sages.

There continues to be a search for wisdom and an effort to identify the sages of our time. By putting ancient and contemporary sages and their wisdom into dialogue with each other, we will understand both past and present better. Who are the sages? What roles do the sages have? Where may we find the sages? These questions, forever asked, will be answered from within a context of dialogue between biblical and contemporary sages, between ancient and modern wisdom.

The chapters in this volume, written over the last decade, represent an attempt to identify characteristics of sages, both ancient and modern, and the wisdom they profess to know and to teach. None of these studies looks at only the ancient sages or only modern ones. Rather, I attempt, through a wide variety of methods and perspectives, to place biblical and modern sages into dialogue with one another or one another's time and place, finding more wisdom and other information forthcoming from these special people than a study of the biblical or the modern exclusively. Finally, since ancient wisdom is only valuable as it is able to speak to us today, and since contemporary wisdom must have some referent to the past in order to understand its nature and function today, such a process, such a dialogue, seems very much in order.

The conclusion contains both a summary of conclusions reached and suggestions for the future study of contemporary wisdom. There are many popular movements that promise wisdom and its benefits (success, longevity, health) to their adherents. Indeed, to cite but one example, the *New York Times* best-seller lists for both fiction (e.g., *The Celestine Prophecy* and its successors) and nonfiction (from *The Road Less Traveled* to *The Prayer of Jabez*) are filled with examples of what our modern culture considers wise and worthy of serious attention. The conclusion asks in what ways ancient biblical wisdom may be able to help us see what really is wise and who the sages are. If, perchance, we choose to reject totally the wisdom of the Bible and the values upon which it is based, at least we should be aware of such a decision and have good reasons for it. The goals of wisdom, both ancient and modern, do not seem to have changed dramatically. The question before us, however, is whether or not the new forms and rhetoric of wisdom in contemporary culture, and the sages who present and teach it, are compatible with sages and wisdom of old. How can the Bible help us answer such questions and help us continue a search for wisdom begun long ago?

It is always an interesting question to consider whether a collection of originally independent studies such as this finally witnesses to something larger than intended by any or all of the individual pieces. Put the classical way, does the whole equal more than the sum of its parts? It would be shortsighted and inappropriate to answer that question at this point. But perhaps to the extent that this volume as a whole pushes toward an even larger task, an even larger dialogue between ancient and modern wisdom and sages, the whole is larger than the sum of its parts. Yet it is only part by part, small piece by small piece, that we can continue such a dialogue. We will never find the perfect sage or the complete wisdom we need for living. But we may be enlivened by the dialogue—textual and social, critical and comparative, imaginative and energizing—in which we are involved. It is the hope of this study of studies, above all other things, that its readers embrace and continue such a dialogue with biblical and contemporary sages and their wisdom in the future.

I.
UNDERSTANDING
BIBLICAL SAGES

CHAPTER 1

From Wisdom to Torah
The Pedagogy of the Sages

What were the *hakamim* of ancient Israel, the wise ones? Were they teachers and scholars? Were they interpreters of experience, authors of aphoristic literature? Were they scribes or sages? Were they interpreters of Torah? Were they masters of hermeneutical rules? What was their role in society? Where did they function? Did they teach in schools? Did they preach in synagogues?

The answers to these and many related questions concerning the *hakamim* are largely dependent upon what period of time we choose to study. If we ask these questions of the biblical period, we get one set of answers.[1] If we ask them of the rabbinic period, we get another.[2] *Hakamim* is a multivalent and ambivalent term.

This chapter was first presented at a meeting of the Society for Old Testament Study, July 1992, in Dublin, Ireland.

1. See R. N. Whybray, *The Intellectual Tradition in the Old Testament*, BZAW 135 (Berlin: Walter de Gruyter, 1974); Andre Lemaire, *Les ecoles et la formation de la Bible dans l'ancient Israel*, OBO 39 (Fribourg: Editions Universitaires; Göttingen: Vandenhoeck & Ruprecht, 1981); John C. Gammie and Leo C. Perdue, eds., *The Sage in Israel and the Ancient Near East* (Winona Lake, Ind.: Eisenbrauns, 1990); and D. W. Jamieson-Drake, *Scribes and Schools in Monarchic Judah*, JSOTSup 109, The Social World of Biblical Antiquity Series 9 (Sheffield: Almond Press, 1991); and James Crenshaw, *Education in Ancient Israel: Across the Deadening Silence* (New York: Doubleday, 1998).

2. See George F. Moore, *Judaism*, 3 vols. (New York: Schocken Books, 1971); and Ephraim E. Urbach, *The Sages, Their Concepts and Beliefs*, 2 vols. (Jerusalem: Magnes Press, 1979).

This chapter explores the relationship between biblical and rabbinic sages. Specifically, we hope to identify the continuity and discontinuity represented by the roles and functions of these wise ones in the postexilic and rabbinic periods of Israel's history. What is new? What creates discontinuity and new functions? What is old? What, if anything, ties the sages of the biblical and rabbinic periods together?

In answering these historical and functional questions, however, we soon discover that contemporary, even confessional, views of the *hakamim* influence us. Our discussion of the sage in ancient Israel begins with the observation that something dramatic and definitive did happen which justifies both a bifurcation between biblical and rabbinic times and which also explains the very different definitions and roles of these figures. Michael Fishbane refers to the events of this time as an "axial development" and characterizes it as a change from scribalism to rabbinicism.[3] Regardless of the terminology, no one debates the significance of this shift for the definition and character of Judaism. A critical demarcation must be made between biblical and rabbinic sages.

Many factors must be considered in evaluating and explaining this change in the nature of sages. Chief among them is the emergence of a Torah-centered community often associated with the reforms of Ezra. There the sage takes center stage as an all-important authority figure, the interpreter of Torah par excellence. The composition of the Hebrew canon, especially Torah and the Prophets, with its normative role for the formation of community and for the identity of Judaism, is surely a critical component. Indeed, the emergence of a Torah-centered Judaism may stand as either a gate or barrier to our study of the sages in these two periods. The newness of this development and its critical function for defining the subsequent nature of Judaism make it difficult to see continuity, to speak of development rather than a change or break. Other contributing factors to a new definition of the sage in rabbinic Judaism include (1) the role of Ezra as *sopher*; (2) Ben Sira's equation of wisdom and Torah (Sir 24:23); (3) the early schools of the rabbis (Hillel, et al.); (4) the influence of Hellenistic civilization, both positively and negatively; and (5) even the teaching of Jesus.[4]

---

3. Michael Fishbane, "From Scribalism to Rabbinicism: Perspectives on the Emergence of Classical Judaism," in Gammie and Perdue, eds., *Sage in Israel*, 439–56.

4. See John J. Collins, *Jewish Wisdom in the Hellenistic Age*, Old Testament Library (Louisville, Ky.: Westminster John Knox, 1997); and Ben Witherington, *Jesus the Sage: The Pilgrimage of Wisdom* (Edinburgh: T&T Clark, 1994).

The new role of a recently completed Torah and the different functions of the sage and rabbi contribute to the division of the ages of the sages—one biblical, the other rabbinic, one devoted to a study of wisdom literature, the other to a study of rabbinic literature. While Ezra is seen as an important precursor of the rabbinic sage, Ben Sira is the transitional figure, both biblical and rabbinic in character. Students of the *hakamim* in the biblical period usually stop with Ben Sira. Students of the *hakamim* in the rabbinic period usually begin with Ben Sira. If we wish to explore both the discontinuity and continuity between biblical and rabbinic sages, we must go through the gate found in Ben Sira and his Torah-centered piety, recognizing the different worlds on each side of the gate but also looking at the common ground upon which late biblical and early rabbinic sages stood. This chapter chooses to do this by examining two very different ways of viewing the roles and significance of the sages in ancient Israel. The first way is found in many classical studies of the rabbinic sages. It emphasizes and highlights the dramatic changes, the discontinuity, the newness in our understanding of these sages in rabbinic Judaism. A second way of presenting and understanding the sages is quite different. Rather than emphasizing a break, its focus is on the continuity of pedagogical role and function in the biblical and rabbinic *hakamim*.

This chapter will compare and contrast the educational agenda of the biblical sages with the sages' role in the development of rabbinic Judaism, finally asking whether these two ways of presenting and understanding the sages and their work are really components of a larger, single story.

From Torah to Wisdom: A Tale of Discontinuity

Highlighting the roles, teaching, and literature of the sages as authoritative interpreters of scripture, especially Torah, is a central purpose for our first way of presenting their history. The period of time surveyed begins with postexilic Israel, especially from Ezra on. Special attention is given to Ben Sira and to the rabbinic literature that culminates with the Mishnah. Indeed, all the talmudic literature provides both a context and evidence for explicating the character and genius of rabbinic Judaism as epitomized in the work of the later sages.

The movement from biblical sage to rabbinic sage begins with biblical wisdom texts as well as some biblical historical texts (Ezra, Nehemiah, 1–2 Chronicles). Later texts such as Ecclesiasticus and

Pirke Abot[5] are also used to describe the character of the sage and the early development of rabbinic schools. Other literary sources, both Jewish and non-Jewish, are used when they provide important historical background (e.g., Josephus) or when they help us to understand the methods of interpretation used by the sages.[6]

The pluralistic nature of society in the period from 200 B.C.E. to 200 C.E. sets the context and is reflected in Jewish, Christian, and other literature produced at this time.[7] This rich literary context underlines the dynamic and ever-changing character of rabbinic interpretation, making it impossible to define Judaism in terms of a dogmatic structure.[8] At the same time, this political, social, and religious pluralism provides a backdrop for understanding the final triumph of Pharisaic Judaism. Though the Pharisees are not reflective of a monochromatic or monolithic interpretation of Tanak and Jewish tradition, a focus on the normative character of the sages and their teachings sometimes creates the impression of a victorious orthodoxy and requires us to choose winners and losers, to view and interpret a pluralistic situation in terms of the religious views of one group. In light of this, there is an unavoidable tension. To present a clear and noncontroversial development of the sages is historically inaccurate.[9] But to suggest that all Jewish interpretation in the period from 200 B.C.E. to 200 C.E. is finally and equally authoritative is also inaccurate, both historically and confessionally. In presenting a picture of the teaching of the sages who became normative for Judaism, it is necessary to make judgments about winners and losers as reflected in and used by the literature of the sages themselves.

In describing the sages, we must distinguish between the *sopher* as scribe, someone interested in textual transmission and accuracy of the biblical text, and as sage, master of hermeneutical rules and interpretation, responsible finally for both midrashim and Mishnah.[10] Scholars assume that from the time of Ben Sira there were schools

5. See R. Travers Herford, ed. and trans., *Pirke Aboth. The Ethics of the Talmud: Sayings of the Fathers* (New York: Schocken Books, 1962).

6. See, e.g., S. Lieberman, *Hellenism in Jewish Palestine* (New York: Jewish Theological Seminary of America, 1950); and David Daube, *Ancient Jewish Law* (Leiden: E. J. Brill, 1981).

7. See J. H. Charlesworth, "Introduction for the General Reader," in *The Old Testament Pseudepigrapha,* ed. J. H. Charlesworth (Garden City, N. Y.: Doubleday, 1983), 1: xxi-xxxiv.

8. Cf., e.g., Donn F. Morgan, *Between Text and Community* (Minneapolis: Fortress Press, 1990), 130ff.

9. See Urbach, *Sages, Their Concepts and Beliefs,* 1:9–11.

10. Ibid., 1:568ff.

where such activities occurred.[11] A primary concern of this way of presenting the sages is not with the process of education and interpretation that occurred in this early rabbinic period but rather with which rabbis were in which schools and with the particular teachings associated with them. Thus, for example, 'Abot will be used to help trace and understand the early rabbis and the content of their teaching, but will not be concerned with the forms of that teaching and the implications for pedagogy contained therein. Moreover, the rabbis most responsible for the shape of the authoritative literary collection (e.g., Akiba and Judah ha-Nasi) will be highlighted.[12]

The hermeneutical rules of Hillel and others take center stage when the process of interpretation found in the sages is presented. No real concern is given to the way in which one teaches a student to become proficient in interpretation. Rather, these well-known methods are discussed in order to show the sages as master interpreters and normative guides. The focus is not usually on particular teaching but on the establishment of an office (i.e., sage) and a method of study and interpretation that continues to be normative to the present day. From Ben Sira onward, the sage is seen as interpreter of scripture par excellence, a person capable of utilizing a number of hermeneutical methods to understand and apply the biblical text to a wide variety of different situations. All of this activity highlights the centrality of Torah for faithful Jewish living, testifying both to the normative nature of Tanak and the interpretations given it by the sage.

Throughout this way of presenting the sages, there is a presumption that these men were special, worthy of attention, and capable of functioning as guides and authoritative interpreters. On what evidence does such a presumption rest? What is the basis of their authority? First, on the basis of his education and study of the biblical text and the teaching of other sages, each sage was an expert, with knowledge of the content of the sacred tradition and of its interpretation. The office of sage/rabbi was not dependent on some official doctrine of inspiration and could theoretically be taken away from one whose teaching was seen to be inadequate. In this sense, the sage's authority rested upon congregational principles. To cite David Daube:

---

11. See, e.g., Sir 51:23: "Draw near to me, you who are untaught, and lodge in my school" (RSV).

12. See, e.g., Moore, *Judaism*, 1:125–60.

The correctness of a decision was guaranteed by the character and learning of him who delivered it. Significantly, the *dibbere sopherim*, "the sayings of the ancient scribes," are never supported by any arguments. The wise man simply knows the true import of a Biblical commandment or the proper supplement to add.[13]

The focus of this characterization of the sages is on content, appropriate teachings, and interpretation. In light of these factors, a particular sage was considered wise and held in esteem. Finally, it is faithful, coherent, and plausible adherence to the Hebrew Scriptures and written and oral tradition, as well as the ability to make sound judgments, that provided the basis of the sages' authority. While a sage should have had a particular lifestyle congruent with community-based values grounded in scripture and tradition, it was his character and his ability to make a sound interpretation that set him apart from others, making him a worthy guide.

Because of the authority associated with the sages, this presentation will highlight teachings and decisions most authoritative for subsequent Judaism.[14] The midrashim and Targumim did not take on as much importance in the ongoing authoritative structures of Judaism created by the sages. Further, when the literature associated with the sages was studied and systematically searched, it was to provide content for particular subjects (e.g., adultery, idolatry) rather than to provide a full and complete picture of the nature of a sage or the ways in which he taught. This is congruent with the ways in which the rabbinic literature itself presents the sages.[15]

This presentation of the sages inevitably begins with Ezra, going quickly to Ben Sira to establish the central place of the *sopher* and the school. Using *Pirke Abot* and other sources, the teaching of the sages is presented up to the Mishnah, comparing and contrasting these teachings with the Sadducees, Essenes, Christians, and others. The final result, if we were to follow the lead of Moore, Urbach, and others, would be a relatively systematic presentation of some very unsystematic material.[16] The genius of the sages and their contribution to the formation of normative, if not systematic, Judaism are highlighted.

---

13. David Daube, "Rabbinic Methods of Interpretation and Hellenistic Rhetoric," *HUCA* 22 (1949): 242.

14. Namely, the halachic material found in the Talmud.

15. See, e.g., the classical treatment of Urbach, *Sages, Their Concepts and Beliefs.*

16. See Moore, *Judaism*; Urbach, *Sages, Their Concepts and Beliefs*; and others.

Throughout, the centrality of Torah study and its necessary application to life would both sustain and testify to the efforts of the sages.

The Sages as Teachers: A Tale of Continuity

A second way of tracing and presenting the development of the sage in ancient Israel focuses on the role of teacher from biblical times through the rabbinic period. The overall concern in this view is continuity. Sources for this presentation differ from our first presentation. Biblical texts, and especially the wisdom literature associated with biblical *hakamim*, play a more important role, with Ezra and the establishment of a Torah-centered community having a lesser role. Ben Sira remains a critical transitional point for understanding the sage and the school, but the relationship of the biblical wisdom tradition to Ben Sira's teachings and the ways in which he continues the biblical wisdom tradition are of central concern here. The secular nature of wisdom, the universalistic worldview, and the focus on experience are highlighted and stressed when examining the antecedents of Ben Sira's teaching.

When the rabbinic material is studied and evaluated, literary wisdom forms (parable, *mashal*) take on special significance. Thus, for example, *Pirke Abot* is important not only because of its references to Hillel and Shammai and its brief history of the early rabbis, but also because of the earlier forms of wisdom teaching contained within it. Midrashim and the aphorisms occurring throughout talmudic literature also receive special attention, since they often provide insights into the ways in which biblical teaching, and even halachic decisions, were actually taught or explained.[17]

The pluralistic literature produced between 200 B.C.E. and 200 C.E. provides an important backdrop for understanding the world in which the sages taught. In this presentation of the sages, less attention is paid to the eventual triumph of Pharisaic Judaism and more to the parallels between aphoristic and instructional literature of all kinds as it witnesses to communities engaged in education.[18] When schools are presented, the references in the sages' writings to different types of educational institutions (e.g., elementary [reading and writing], Bible, Mishnah, and Talmud) become important. Though the role

---

17. See, e.g., H. I. Marrou, *A History of Education in Antiquity* (Madison, Wis.: University of Wisconsin Press, 1982), 314ff.

18. See Collins, *Jewish Wisdom.*

of sages within these institutions remains unclear, the importance of education does not. If the nature and existence of schools in biblical Israel is a matter of supposition, this is not the case after Ben Sira.[19] Throughout this presentation, the *process* of education (pedagogy, the asking of questions, the aphoristic forms, the appeal to experience) receives much attention.

In presenting the teaching of the sages, parallels are drawn between the moral nature and teachings of biblical wisdom and rabbinic literature. The experiential basis of the sages is also an important part of the educational continuum between Bible and rabbi. It would probably be incorrect to assume that the normative nature of Torah did not supply a touchstone for the *hakamim* of the rabbinic period, but this was integrated into wise living, as with Ben Sira and those before him.[20] Thus, a focus on the sages as teachers and educators stresses the process of teaching and its results viewed from the perspective of wisdom and knowledge, versus a particular reading of Torah and the tradition.

When the authority of the sage is addressed, wisdom and its teachings again become important. G. F. Moore characterized the importance of Hillel in the following manner:

> Hillel, of all the rabbis, is the most familiar name to most Christians. He owes this reputation to the anecdotes which illustrate his genial temper and to the fine religious and moral aphorisms that are quoted from him; but his great significance in the history of Judaism lies not so much in these things as in the new impulse and direction he gave to the study of the law, the new spirit he infused into Pharisaism.[21]

In contrast to Moore's approach, this presentation of the sage as teacher focuses on Hillel's teachings and their relationship to an ongoing activity of the biblical and rabbinic sage as epitomized in aphoristic sayings, rather than stressing the new or normative spirit. The character of the sages and teachers as described in rabbinic materials are placed in dialogue and continuity with the character of the biblical *hakamim*. Here Ben Sira provides an all-important connection,

---

19. See Marrou, *History of Education;* Whybray, *Intellectual Tradition*; and Crenshaw, *Education in Ancient Israel.*

20. "[T]heir influence was not due to charisma but to their wisdom; and this wisdom implies knowledge of the Torah and Halakha and absolute faithfulness to their injunctions and principles" (Urbach, *Sages, Their Concepts and Beliefs,* 1:571).

21. Moore, *Judaism,* 1:81.

for he is often seen as the last of the biblical *hakamim* and the first of the sages of later times.[22]

The historical framework for presenting this picture of teaching and education begins deep within the biblical period. Though the institutions that support such activities are usually only vaguely described, literature reflecting the values and ideals of the *hakamim* does exist. Surely Ezra is important here, for the Torah-centered community he helped to create is at least partially an explanation for the teaching of Ben Sira. The schools that provide the educational locus for post–Ben Sira Israel continue to use both the literary methods of biblical sages and many of their values (e.g., experience, universalism, wisdom). The marriage of wisdom and Torah in Ben Sira is not only new but also reflects continuity—as a way for wisdom to live on in the teaching methods and character of the rabbinic sage. Indeed, the later *hakamim*, the sages, are not only steeped in Torah but wise in the ways of the world. It is that wisdom and its embrace of all facets of human experience that is a part of their authority and helps to define the ways in which they will carry out their teaching.

Explication and Analysis

I have presented two very different ways of understanding the significance of the sage in ancient Israel from biblical to rabbinic times. Both look seriously at certain aspects of the sages, one focusing on discontinuity and newness, and one focusing on continuity and common concerns shared by the wise. One way is well known to us, the second is less so. What are we to do with all of this? Both discontinuity and the new, and continuity and the common are potentially valuable. But does the evidence itself warrant a focus on one rather than the other?

Any presentation of the sage in ancient Israel must take seriously the factor of discontinuity. Biblical sages are not rabbinic sages. Something has happened, an axial development, if you will. The tension created by this change cannot be erased. The role and teaching associated with rabbinic sages is associated with a new norm, a new authority. Like Jesus for Christians, the words, activities, and role of

---

22. Ben Sira is not officially viewed as a rabbi or a part of the rabbinic tradition, but for the many reasons given in this chapter he is cited and referred to by both biblical wisdom scholars and rabbinic scholars as standing in the middle, pointing both forward and backward. His explicit reference to sages and his equation of Torah with traditional wisdom are two of the many reasons for this special placement.

the rabbinic sages are authoritative in a new way, a way that colors the shape and interpretation of Tanak forever. The bifurcation between biblical sage and rabbinic sage, between Moses and Hillel, between written and oral tradition, makes discontinuity or normative differentiation a central part of their story and justifiably warrants the term "axial change." For any presentation of the sages not to recognize this phenomenon, for both ancient Israel and the present day, is to misrepresent them and their significance.

But while the norms associated with rabbinic and talmudic sages are signals of discontinuity at one level, is there not continuity at others? My second way of presenting the sages, with its focus on wisdom, on common literary forms (aphorisms), on common characteristics of biblical and rabbinic sages as teacher or educators, stresses such continuity. Without denying the normative nature of rabbinic teaching and the new norms associated with it, I have tried to find a common denominator associated with the *hakamim* of both biblical and rabbinic times. In one sense, such a common endeavor, teaching, and education would appear to be banal. Does not every society care about these things? Does not every society have and use aphorism and value experience in formulating present and future behavioral patterns? Yet, as Lieberman, Stern, and others have shown, the rabbinic sages adapted and used Greek and Roman secular aphoristic literature in ways distinctive to their own, particular, Torah-centered piety.[23] The common and popular wisdom of the rabbinic sages' time was not accepted without careful and significant changes. The normativeness of Torah, as conceived and interpreted by the sages, was an all-important medium through which whatever it meant to teach, to be wise, must pass.

This study suggests there were many things associated with what it meant to be wise. What it meant to learn and what it meant to live faithfully formed a continuum within Israel's sacred tradition. Here again, the figure and writings of Ben Sira become all important. To say that wisdom is Torah if found in the mouth of Rabbi Akiba is a notion capable of being evaluated solely in terms of the rabbinic teaching and piety of his time. Not so with Ben Sira. The newness of Ben Sira's teaching makes little or no sense without a careful and binding connection between biblical aphoristic literature and the new Torah piety of his day. It has been amply demonstrated that the notion Torah equals wis-

---

23. Cf. references in note 7 above.

dom has been a significant perspective from which to view earlier biblical literature.[24] But we must also look forward, understanding the nature of the sage, Torah, and the educational endeavors of rabbinic times in light of their connection to biblical wisdom, as Ben Sira himself has done. In one sense, the rabbis are like Ben Sira: involved in the same endeavor as the biblical *hakamim*, involved in the education of Israel, involved in the teaching of wisdom and its living.

Two ways to view the work of the sages of ancient Israel are set before us. One way stresses the new perspectives of the rabbis and uses Tanak as a backdrop, focusing on discontinuity. The other way uses the Bible to explain the methods and task of all sages, and focuses on the continuity of a common educational endeavor. Must we choose?

One or Two Stories?

How shall we tell the story of the sages of biblical and rabbinic times? The choice we make about how to present the sages of Israel, what material we will focus upon and value, depends greatly upon our purpose. If, for example, we are biblical or rabbinic scholars, we usually pay closest attention to the subjects in our own fields, having neither time nor inclination to go further, to make connections with a literature and history relatively unknown to us. In addition, religious and confessional norms (e.g., the authority ascribed to biblical versus rabbinic sages) also divide our periods and subjects of study and make an attempt to make connections more difficult. To the extent that we try to bridge the gap between biblical and rabbinic sages, we will be affected by a pressure to recognize the new, the different, the distinctive. It is difficult to jump over the chasm represented by Ben Sira and by the normativeness of subsequent sages, but the continuity of the *hakamim* in both periods seems to hold a promise. If we search for a common thread that ties the sages together, education and aphoristic speech (with all of its biblical characteristics, its universalism, its secular emphasis, experience, and morality) seem to offer serious possibilities. The whole story cannot be told with this focus, but it is part of the story, and one largely neglected to this point.

At the end of an essay on the sages, John Gammie makes the following point: "Despite necessary particularistic elements in all religious traditions, the sages may function—should they choose—not

---

24. See, e.g., Gerald Sheppard, *Wisdom as a Hermeneutical Construct*, BZAW 151 (New York: Walter de Gruyter, 1980).

only as builders of houses but also as builders of bridges."[25] The sages we study and think on today are dead and gone. Consequently, I would add one slight emendation to Gammie's observation. The sages may function, should *we* choose, as builders of bridges. Should *we* do this, through a focus on education or some other common tie, it will still be a story filled with discontinuity and newness, but hopefully with some strong common thread that binds all of us into the activities and wisdom of the sages, both biblical and rabbinic.

---

25. John C. Gammie, "From Prudentialism to Apocalypticism: The Houses of the Sages amid the Varying Forms of Wisdom," in Gammie and Purdue, eds., *Sage in Israel*, 497.

CHAPTER 2

Confucius, Solomon, and Their Literature
The Making of Sages

The purpose of this chapter is to explore the nature of the relationship between sages and the literature associated with them. Although many important comparative studies focusing on the nature of sages have been completed in the past,[1] the ways in which the scriptures or authoritative literature associated with these figures contribute to their social functions as sages is rarely a topic of investigation. The methods presupposed in this brief chapter are intentionally programmatic, comparative, and dialogical. As a programmatic piece, more questions will be raised than answered. One hoped-for result of this chapter is to provoke and entice others with far more specific knowledge to explore some of the questions raised.

This chapter is comparative in the sense that it places two sages with very different cultural and religious histories side by side. No suggestion is made about historical connections between these two sages, Confucius and Solomon, who lived several hundred years and several worlds apart. Nevertheless, there are some common elements best seen by looking at the scriptures associated with Confucius and

---

1. See the essays in Part I of John C. Gammie and Leo C. Purdue, eds., *The Sage in Israel and the Ancient Near East* (Winona Lake, Ind.: Eisenbrauns, 1990); Sung-Hae Kim, *The Righteous and the Sage: A Comparative Study on the Ideal Images of Man in Biblical Israel and Classical China* (Seoul: Sogang University Press, 1985); and Julia Chang, *Confucianism and Christianity: A Comparative Study* (Tokyo: Kodansha International, 1977).

Solomon that deserve serious consideration as we contemplate the nature of sages and their societal functions.

This chapter is intentionally dialogical in its method. It presupposes that authoritative texts and communities that use them are in some type of regular dialogue at a variety of different levels (e.g., family, gathered worshiping body, state, society). Both Confucius and Solomon can best and most fully be understood as sages when this dialogical nature of their communities, epitomized by the scriptures associated with them, is taken with utmost seriousness.

The motivation and importance for studying the ancient sages Confucius and Solomon stems not only from a desire to understand ancient China or ancient Israel. Rather, sages have been major carriers of value for society in times past. In a contemporary period characterized by a plurality of value claims and no clear direction or distinction between right and wrong, good and bad, looking to sages or other figures like them is not an act of disinterested scholarship. But if we are to find and learn from contemporary sages, we must first understand how sages function in culture. Studying the scriptures associated with sages is a small part of that process.

Confucius is a part of this study because one of my own contexts for study of the sages has been Asia. Limited time, knowledge, and exposure to the sapiential traditions of Asia tempt me to qualify everything I say about sages in that part of the world. Instead, I have chosen to make broad and general observations and comparisons that I hope will be both provocative and helpful to those who study Confucius and other Asian sages seriously.

A Thesis and an Irony

The particular pictures of sages as derived from literature written by or about them is not the concern of this chapter. Whether or not Confucius or Solomon were actually sages is only of secondary importance. We begin instead with the assertion that both Confucius and Solomon were and are sages because the literature associated with these men, written or composed before, during, and after their lifetimes says or assumes they were sages. This assumption leads us to the thesis of this chapter: Sages in general, and Confucius and Solomon in particular, are social constructs. The evidence for this thesis is the vast body of authoritative literature, most of it not compiled or written by either Confucius or Solomon but attributed to them. Put another way, Confucius and Solomon do not exist as sages without the literature that says they are such and that then gives examples of their sagacity.

We must examine this thesis with reference to the scriptures associated with both Confucius and Solomon, but a few general observations are in order first. To say that sages are social constructs assumes a body or group that accomplishes the task of constructing. Sages are most often constructed by families, religious institutions, schools (or special places of learning), and states or other large civic entities. The purposes of the social constructs associated with sages are varied but usually have to do with social control and direction. Affirmation of basic values and systems of morality are often a part of the social constructs associated with sages, and stability and order are the hoped-for result.[2] Finally, for the sage to become effective for the social group, a literature is often compiled and associated with the sage, his disciples, and followers.[3] This literature becomes normative, affirming the specific teachings of the sage, but, perhaps just as important, carries and proclaims traditions which maintain that Solomon and Confucius are sages. This literature may contain writings that actually precede the life and work of the sage, writings that represent the sage's actual teaching, and literature written after the lifetime of the sage.

On the basis of our thesis, we might assume that to find the real Confucius or Solomon, all that is necessary is to locate the social group responsible for the construction of each man as a sage. Even if that were possible, however, the particular relationship between the construct of the sage in authoritative literature and the groups that are responsible for and affected by this construct is subject to at least two different developments that have ironic twists or outcomes. On the one hand, once the sage is constructed, the wisdom associated with that sage is capable of transcending the intentions of the community that calls Confucius or Solomon a sage. The wisdom of Solomon or Confucius becomes public property, with no strict control over its interpretation. Though initially concerned with social control and stability, it is perfectly possible for the construct of the sage to be used to overturn or criticize the very social system it was intended to support. In this case, the text is used to shape the community in new ways.

---

2. Notice that the proclamation of the identity of a particular institution is not usually associated with the sages but is instead to be found in other institutional roles.

3. Oral tradition can also affirm a sage's standing, but in the case of Confucius and Solomon we are primarily interested in the literary deposit that is the foundation for their social functions as sages.

On the other hand, almost the exact opposite of this is also possible. In creating a literature associated with the sage, one of the apparent intentions was to freeze the words of the sage, to say there is no more, or no better, wisdom to be gotten from Solomon or Confucius. Ironically, the textual dialogue with the community created by this freezing process provides the possibility for broadening and changing interpretations and applications while keeping faithful to the normative textual traditions. In this case, the community continues to shape the text through its subsequent interpretations.[4]

In summary, the institution chooses or elevates or canonizes sages, creating social constructs for particular purposes and finalizing this process with bodies of literature associated with them. Ironically, however, once this process has occurred, the institution can no longer necessarily control the picture of the sages created. The dialogue between sapiential literature and communities searching for knowledge, with the mandate and authority of Confucius and Solomon as sages, reflects the fact that wisdom permeates everything. Wisdom is and will be found and applied to far more than what the original constructors of these sages intended.

How did this happen? How is it reflected in the literature itself? What does all of this tell us about developments in biblical and Asian traditions that have occurred since the time of the original construction of the sage?

Solomon, Confucius, and Their Scriptures: Developmental Sketches

The social construction of the sages Confucius and Solomon required collecting materials concerned with wisdom and associating these materials with these figures. This was not done in a way that implied Solomon and Confucius were authors of all this material. Rather, the appropriate analogue might be the biblical David, who as a singer is associated with all of the psalms; whether or not he wrote all of them is quite beside the point. Such a distinction between actual authorship and association because of wisdom suggests that the group that is connecting Solomon or Confucius with particular literature already has a strong notion of their sage-like qualities. Put another way, the

---

4. The writings of Brevard Childs on canon often focus on the interaction between text and community, with each being shaped by the other in different ways. See, for example, his Introduction to the Old Testament as Scripture (Philadelphia: Fortress, 1978), where he gives examples for each biblical book of its subsequent interpretation by communities of faith.

decision to regard Solomon as a sage precedes the attribution to him of many writings which themselves seemingly demonstrate that Solomon is a sage. Indeed, perhaps, this is not the function of this literature at all. Rather, because we consider, for whatever reasons, Confucius or Solomon to be sages, we approach their writings as wisdom, with all of the authority appropriately accorded to it.

The biblical literature pertinent for understanding Solomon as a sage is of two kinds: the narrative in 1 Kings 3–4 describing Solomon's great wisdom given to him by God, and the wisdom literature of Proverbs and Ecclesiastes.[5] Proverbs and Ecclesiastes contain the vast majority of the wisdom of Solomon in the Bible. Whether or not the stories in 1 Kings reflect a later attribution of wisdom to Solomon, or are indicative of the basis upon which subsequent collections were associated with Solomon, is a matter of debate in biblical scholarship, but one that does not affect the goals of this study.[6]

The book of Proverbs clearly contains aphoristic literature from at least two different social loci: the family, sometimes referred to as popular wisdom,[7] and monarchial wisdom, usually associated with royal counselors and perhaps, sometimes, the king himself. All students of this literature posit that some popular wisdom precedes the monarchy itself and surely is not to be originally attributed to Solomon. Moreover, some of the royal wisdom is attributed by scholarship to Egyptian provenance and to several different monarchial reigns in ancient Israel. There continues to be much debate over whether the explicitly theological wisdom so prevalent in Proverbs 1–9 is early or late, but we can safely assume that some of the wisdom in Proverbs, theological or not, was surely composed and collected long after Solomon was considered to be a sage. The book of Ecclesiastes, while containing popular proverbs that may have been written much earlier, was clearly composed long after Solomon's reign and is in all probability the result of the social construct already present in both Proverbs and 1 Kings 3–4.

---

5. The Song of Songs is sometimes considered to be wisdom literature primarily because of its attribution to Solomon the sage. But for the purposes of this essay we will not consider the problematic relationship between the Song and wisdom literature.

6. See R. B. Y. Scott, "Solomon and the Beginnings of Wisdom in the Bible," in *Studies in Ancient Israelite Wisdom*, ed. J. L. Crenshaw (New York: KTAV Publishing House, 1976), 84–101. For our present purposes, however, an examination of the wisdom literature of the Hebrew Bible will adequately demonstrate the relationship and development pertaining to Solomon's wisdom.

7. Popular wisdom is also sometimes distinguished from family wisdom. But one compelling argument would suggest that family wisdom probably had to become popular in order to circulate widely enough to be included in scriptural collections.

The compositional history of wisdom literature and its relationship to the social construction of Solomon as sage is difficult to trace precisely because of the anonymity of the collectors who, by and large, are content to have their wisdom associated with Solomon. Notable exceptions to this are the sayings of Agur (Prov 30:1–33) and Lemuel (Prov 31:1–9). Even here, however, the inclusion of this wisdom has to be connected with Solomon, whose writings make up the vast majority of the collection.

It would appear that first there was popular/family wisdom, circulating within the society much as it does today, in aphoristic, usually poetic, forms. In all probability, royal wisdom was also circulating, some of it borrowed from Egypt and elsewhere.[8] At some point after Solomon's death, much of this wisdom was associated with and attributed to the wise king who, as reflected in 1 Kings 3–4 had become a sage. Through a compositional history subject to many debates in terms of the details, the books of Proverbs and Ecclesiastes reached their final form sometime in the postexilic period, fully five hundred years or more after the death of Solomon. Of the two wisdom books, Ecclesiastes probably reflects a composition over a much shorter period of time, mainly in the postexilic period itself. On the other hand, the collecting of wisdom in Proverbs began before Solomon and was accelerated and given direction and shape as the central figure of the sage as author or epitome of the wise man (father/king) was constructed. The Song of Songs, though not wisdom literature in the same sense as that of Proverbs and Ecclesiastes,[9] is also dependent upon the Solomonic social construct. This is a demonstration of the way the figure of sage can be used to carry many different types of values for the society, even ones not originally associated with wisdom.

The literature associated with Confucius as sage is a bit clearer in its provenance, even if its precise dating alludes us. The Five Classics and Four Books will be the focus for the purposes of this essay.[10] It is generally agreed that some of the aphoristic material contained in these books has a provenance that predates Confucius. Moreover, some of this material has been assumed to have a royal origin, either king or royal advisors, and some has a popular origin that is separate from the institution of the state or monarchy. Although it is very dif-

---

8. Notice the parallels between the Egyptian "Instruction of Amen-em-ope" and Prov 22:17–24:22.

9. See, e.g., Roland Murphy's writings on this book.

10. See Chang, *Confucianism and Christianity*, xviii.

ficult to determine materials to be associated with the real Confucius, no one doubts that some of this literature is from his time. There is a great deal of debate, however, about whether Confucius should be seen as a collector of previous wisdom or the originator of new wisdom.[11] In any case, the development depicted by this literature suggests the following sequence. First, there existed wisdom of both a popular and royal nature, some already collected in an indeterminate form. Second, Confucius himself and his immediate followers collected this wisdom and used it to discuss and justify certain modes of behavior and allegiances (e.g., fivefold relationships, the state as locus for action). They may even have been responsible for identifying and labeling some of this material as wisdom. Third, later generations further collected and added to this record of Confucius's work, sometimes attributing new material to him and sometimes to disciples (e.g., Mencius) who followed in his stead. This process of collection and recollection, of sifting and refining old wisdom and adding new wisdom, as with Solomon, continued for many centuries. However, from the time of Confucius himself, this sage became the center point of the collecting process, tying the old together with the new under the rubric of Confucius the wise. The fact that Confucius himself said he is not a sage emphasizes the social construct of sage, that a sage is made by persons other than the sage himself. The resultant picture of wisdom, centered on Confucius, is (1) a series of "classics" that are authoritative for the sage par excellence and precede him, followed by, (2) his own wisdom, followed by (3) the wisdom of his disciples.

General Observations and Points in Common

Solomon and Confucius share several points in common. Wisdom existed in China and Israel before Confucius and Solomon. Such an observation provides an opportunity to identify the source of some of the wisdom attributed to each sage. More importantly, it calls us to recognize a social locus and an already existent social construction for wisdom that may be subsumed under the new construction associated with these two sages (family/clan, popular culture, monarchy, school). In other words, the collection of materials around these sages represents an amalgamation of previous social constructs and loci.

---

11. For a discussion of the relationship of Confucius to the classics, see John B. Henderson, *Scripture, Canon, and Commentary: A Comparison of Confucian and Western Exegesis* (Princeton, N.J.: Princeton University Press, 1991), 21–37.

Unfortunately, there are no records that reflect the choosing of Solomon or Confucius to be sages. The following criteria would seem to be necessary, however. First, there must be a cultural valuing of wisdom. This is testified to by both cultures. Second, the sage must be associated with some office or function for which the attribution of wisdom seems both credible and legitimate. A king, a family head, a teacher, or someone to whom is attributed a special place in the culture is necessary. Third, the wisdom of the sage must be demonstrable by words that reflect reason, special insight, teaching ability, and special choosing by God or some other transcendent source. Finally, there must be a social group that has a stake, something to gain or to uphold or to conserve by attributing wisdom to the particular sage. The sage is then chosen for purposes of social control. However, the characteristics of the sage that led to his being chosen may not necessarily be identical with the social group that makes him sage. So, for example, the final construction of Solomon as sage and king is accomplished in a time when there is no kingship in Israel. Or again, Confucius as master teacher is associated with the state and its organization even though the sage himself is hardly a good representative of full and active involvement in such a social system. The sage's actual life situation must be compatible with the social system that constructs the sage. This is determined not by the sage but by the institutions that view him as such.

The significance of the construction of sages can be found also in wisdom literature's portrayal of wisdom. For Solomon especially but also Confucius, wisdom in its most important and authoritative form is to be attributed to the sage himself. In the case of Solomon, we have seen that all previous and later wisdom is collected around this social construct. In the case of Confucius, although he cites the authorities of previous wisdom (e.g., the Odes), it is clear that this authority is dependent upon his citation, that is, upon the authority resident in the construction of Confucius as sage. Consequently, in this literature there is a reversal of the actual process of attaining and giving wisdom. The process of collecting wisdom was dependent upon earlier aphorisms, knowledge of advisors, popular culture, previous kings, and so on. But now it is all centered in Solomon and Confucius, as if wisdom began with them.

The stories about Confucius throughout the Four Books and the narrative of Solomon's wisdom in 1 Kings 3–4 reflect a knowledge of each man's wisdom that is circulated among the people. Whether this came before, during, or after the process of becoming a sage is difficult to determine. Nevertheless, the presence of these stories may be considered an important component for the success of the social construct. While kings and good teachers may be considered sages in some *ex officio* sense in both Chinese and Israelite cultures, to become as important and central as Confucius and Solomon requires more than being just an excellent teacher or a powerful and wise king. The presence of an authoritative narrative thus reflects an important corroborative element vital to the construct itself. Whether this was done intentionally by the monarchy or by the followers of the sage is really beside the point. It turned out to be a vital ingredient in the process.

The compilation of a literature associated with these two sages at some point reached official completion. At that point, the wisdom of Confucius and Solomon was frozen. The literature itself continues to be preserved faithfully and to be transmitted to those who need or want it. Ironically, the process of freezing, which ostensibly limits the words of the sage, also creates the possibility for the words to be public and universal. In this way, others who have been put in charge of these words can exercise social control.

The sage as social construct is not the state, not the religious establishment, not the school, and not the family. Rather, the sage is to be used in the service of these social realities, to help reflect their values, concerns, and hierarchical structures. As we seek to describe the public domain into which Solomon and Confucius function as the wise, we must ask who is in control of the literature and how those groups relate to the overall social and power configurations in society. The fact that these groups change but the words of the sages do not tells us something important about the sage and his literature. On the one hand, the sapiential literature is malleable. No matter how rigid the moral teachings contained therein may seem, they are in fact capable of being utilized and lived in a wide variety of settings. When this rich history of the life of the sage and his literature is viewed as a whole, it must be affirmed that indeed the words of Confucius and Solomon belong to the world, to the public, to the culture. Their wisdom is not, finally, the property of any given social group, though the social constructs of the sages need at least one or more of these groups at any given time to continue to live.

Finally, when examining the sages Solomon and Confucius as social constructs, searching for the original words of the sage, and sometimes even finding them, is only a small part of the picture. Surely we must continue to try and understand the compositional history of the literature associated with these sages. To the extent that we do, we may know more of the construction process that finally led to the powerful influence each of these figures has as a sage. On the other hand, as we have seen, much of this process is anonymous. Further, those who benefit most from the social construction may be found in places far removed from the literature's original setting, for example, the cult. Viewed in this way, searching for and discussing the sage as social construct may deal more with the aftereffects of the process and less with the actual construction and compositional history. That history is shrouded in uncertainty and contains many anonymous voices coming from across cultures and times far removed from the biblical sages.

Sages and Their Life after Scripture

Solomon and Confucius continue to be important in a number of different religious and cultural contexts. The best explanation for this phenomenon, given the historical vicissitudes of China, Israel, and many other settings where the influence of these sages has been and continues to be felt, rests in the phenomenon of dialogue. This is a dialogue between the authoritative texts associated with these sages and a community that continues to want to understand its values and its wisdom in relationship to those texts. In order for this dialogue to continue into the present day, there must be (1) a social locus for the text and (2) an affirmation of the need for wisdom as it has been associated with Solomon and Confucius and their respective wisdom literature. The dialogue itself will in all probability produce other texts, other authorities that reflect contemporary priorities and truths, but each of these dialogues with the sages always has as its basis some reference to the texts that first and foremost hold up the sage as social construct. This does not mean the subsequent teachings associated with Solomon or Confucius are not finally more important in terms of commanding assent or addressing the contemporary issues than the old texts. Rather, the old texts retain a vital function by their special placement within the culture. After over two millennia, the sagehood of both Solomon and Confucius is more than the property of any given social group; it belongs also to the cultures that continue to have the texts of these sages and to be influenced by their wisdom.

The historical and cultural adventures in which Solomonic and Confucian writings take part are very different. In the Confucian tradition, despite many different phases and many different schools, Confucius as a sage continues to be central. In some ways, it looked as if this might happen in the ancient Near East with Solomon as well. Indeed, the Wisdom of Solomon and other writings, written long after the official literature was completed and reflecting a pseudonymous Solomonic wisdom, pointed toward a development that might have been even more comprehensive than Confucianism. But, in fact, Solomon to a certain extent appears to recede into the background of normative rabbinic Judaism. Solomon is not as central a figure today as he was in the postexilic period, though the dialogue between his literature and contemporary culture continues to occur.[12]

It is helpful at this point to explore some of the differences between these two wisdom traditions, their sages, and their literature. Some have suggested that the difference between the sages of Confucianism and Judaism concerns the nature of the revelation from God. This observation does not appear to take seriously enough the transcendent nature of Confucius's wisdom nor the experiential authority of much of Solomon's wisdom. Nevertheless, it does rest on an observation made about both of these sages, namely, that as social constructs their values and authority must be found not only in the literature about and attributed to them but also with the groups who need and want and use them as sages. In the case of Judaism there can be no doubt that a revelatory religious perspective is to be associated with one of the first and most important social loci in which the completed writings of Solomon functioned, namely, the Jewish community in Jerusalem of Ezra and Nehemiah. Moreover, that community, with its Torah centrality, coupled with the pictures of sages reflected in the later writings of Jesus ben Sira, represented what Michael Fishbane has called an axiological development in the history of the Jewish people.[13] That development, coming to life in rabbinic Judaism and oral Torah, produced sages who were now wise in relationship to their knowledge of Torah and their ability to interpret it faithfully for the people. As with Jesus for Christians, so the revealed Torah is the centerpiece of Judaism, and all must be related to its values. Torah, to that extent, becomes the sapiential literature par excellence, the wisdom of God, though never to the exclusion of Solomon, Proverbs, and other wisdom. In light of this study, however, this

---

12. The fact that wisdom and Torah were not related explicitly until Ben Sira may help to explain this development. That is, the Torah-centered Judaism and its subsequent authoritative writings were already influenced by a separation of wisdom from Torah and Prophets before Ben Sira. See chapter 1.

13. See Michael Fishbane, "From Scribalism to Rabbinicism," in Gammie and Purdue, eds., *Sage in Israel*, 439–56.

axiological development needed more than the centrality of Torah; it also needed a vehicle to carry and transmit the Torah's values. That carrier and transmitter was the social construct of Solomon, which was then given to Ben Sira and then to the rabbis, on through the present. So, though Solomon and his literature have left center stage, the construct created by that literature continues to be there, albeit now with other literature to interpret.

Is it possible, even probable, that we might see the same kind of development in contemporary China? To what extent, for example, does the wisdom of Mao depend upon the existence of a social construct long associated with Confucius in order to command the allegiance of the people? If not in terms of content, what about as a carrier or transmitter? Does Mao not need the precedent and the long-standing tradition of the sage, so centrally associated with Confucius?[14]

This chapter has been a general story of two sages and the two social constructions they represent for two very different cultures. I have stressed primarily the points they share in common. But the full stories of Confucius and Solomon are anchored in the particular cultures to which they belong. While it is true that they have become public property, their stories are finally stories of the particular and not the general. But those stories, which have been told often and well by many, tell of a growth of tradition, of wisdom associated with both sages. How would the original sages and those responsible for their construction feel about all of this? Perhaps the best yardstick might be the answer to the question, "Is the search for wisdom now congruent with what the sages said we must care about?" The answer, probably both yes and no, is itself reflective of a lively dialogue and debate about the world, its order and meaning. Solomon and Confucius might well be happy with such an answer.

Cathedrals and Sages: An Analogical Metaphor

Think for a moment of the cathedral,[15] the large church that has central importance in a particular ecclesiastical region. Many cathedrals are grand buildings, awe-inspiring in size, in the intricacy of detail in

---

14. On the grounds of the old Confucian Temple in Beijing is a small display of the twentieth-century Communist military. Why it is there I am not sure, but the juxtaposition of two very important carriers of value and tradition, one old, one new, is intriguing.

15. One could easily think of a temple, a large parish church, or another analogue to the cathedral that serves some of the same functions and has some of the same characteristics.

stone work, in the beauty of their stained-glass windows, and in their many other characteristics that they possess and few normal parish churches do. When one looks at a cathedral as a building, it sometimes gives the impression of anonymity. Most cathedrals are built over many generations, and it is not always easy to identify a particular architect's work, though often a cathedral tries to continue the style with which it was begun. But, over the years, many things are added to the original plans while some things are taken away; it becomes difficult to determine which is which—what is original and what is not, what was intended from the beginning and what was not. In short, a cathedral is difficult to date. There is a style, but the lasting impression is of a building that is the work of many, usually over a long period. It is almost always impossible to determine when the building actually began unless there is a cornerstone, and these are sometimes unreliable.

What was there before the cathedral? Where did the materials to build it come from? Even if we are speaking of a modern cathedral, where there are records kept, there is rarely any one person who has lived long enough and been involved with all facets of the work to be able to answer these questions. Truly the cathedral is representative of the aphorism that the whole is greater than the sum of its parts. That which speaks most eloquently and best for the cathedral is the cathedral itself.

The cathedral, both in its rich history of construction as well as in its life as a centrally placed institution in the midst of its particular culture, represents a dialogue between religious tradition and politics, both local and national, and culture. This occurs in the choice of architectural styles as well as in the conception of the cathedral's mission to its society. The cathedral building almost always represents a mixture of old and new, for something is always being replaced or added. Sometimes an old style is copied in the hopes of replacing earlier work with identical contemporary work, but it is never quite the same. Sometimes new art and new designs are incorporated into the midst of older ones, with pleasing and not so pleasing effects on worshipers and visitors.

The cathedral represents a long history that is never quite complete. With its congregation composed of some locals and many visitors, with its programs directed at the local community and also to the church at large, the cathedral represents the local and the particular as well as the universal, and it holds these in tension. Its appearance and style cannot help but reflect the local culture out of which it comes. But the scope and size and the other larger-than-life dimensions of the cathedral point to universal realities shared by worshiping Christians with the culture as a whole. In this sense, cathedrals are value carriers not simply of the Christian faith but also of the culture.

Cathedrals, then, are transcendent; they point beyond themselves. In this process of pointing beyond themselves, they are multivalent. For some, they point to God in a very Christian form. For others, they point to the political life of the community, the state, and the country. For still others, they point to the culture in which the cathedral is found and which it represents in majestic and sometimes eclectic characteristics added over a long period of time.

Is a cathedral, like a sage, a social construct? Yes. But it is finally frail and finite, capable of losing all of what it possesses the moment a bomb drops. On the other hand, the cathedral also symbolizes an activity, a building process that stems finally from the faith of a great many people and even the society's complicity, if not always affirmation of the faith, in the process. This process continues in the building and rebuilding of particular cathedrals should they happen to be destroyed. This process continues with new cathedrals in other places that are, whether they know it or not, dependent upon the earlier processes represented by the old cathedrals.

So it is also with the sages and the wisdom they search for, in particular for us, Confucius and Solomon. Like a cathedral, it is almost impossible to determine when the social construction of these mythic sages began or to identify exactly who did what to create them. All we have is the sage and the process of searching for wisdom reflected in the texts given authority by the community. That wisdom, and the figure of the sage associated with it, can and will be debunked, banned, forgotten at times. But the search that the sage as social construct represents, the values proclaimed and carried—that search goes on, and so, therefore, do Solomon and Confucius, even to the present day.

CHAPTER 3

Educational Roles and Pedagogical Methods
Teaching Wisdom and Creation in Proverbs

Biblical wisdom has much to say to our contemporary society. In order to listen to wisdom's message, however, we must not only discern a definition of wisdom but also determine how wisdom was taught. Insights of contemporary educational theorists, speaking to the issues of contemporary society, can help in a search for understanding the functions of the sages, the teachers of wisdom, in ancient Israel.

How might the sages of ancient Israel have taught about the figure of Wisdom and creation? What does the teacher who uses Proverbs look like? How are the figure of Wisdom and creation used for didactic purposes? What are the educational methods and goals of those who had Proverbs as part of their instructional repertoire? How can contemporary educational theory be related to biblical literature and to the tasks of the sages? While these questions have received some attention in biblical scholarship,[1] new perspectives can shed light on them.[2] By examining the interrelationship of ancient and contemporary educational agendas, we can discover more about the biblical

---

An earlier version of this chapter was presented at the national meeting of the Society of Biblical Literature in Anaheim, California, in 1989. While the original focus was on Proverbs 1–9, this has been expanded and changed significantly in the present version.

1. See, e.g., Leo Purdue, *Wisdom and Creation* (Nashville: Abingdon Press, 1994); and Claudia V. Camp, *Wisdom and the Feminine in the Book of Proverbs*, Bible and Literature Series 2 (Sheffield: Almond Press, 1985).

2. See, however, M. Fox, "The Pedagogy of Proverbs," *JBL* 113 (1994): 233–43; and James Crenshaw, *Education in Ancient Israel: Across the Deadening Silence* (New York: Doubleday, 1998).

sage and understand biblical wisdom literature's educational role in contemporary society. My overall purpose is to provoke further thought about biblical wisdom literature and its educational role in our present society, while learning more of the biblical sages.

Modern biblical scholarship of Proverbs has focused primarily on literary, historical, and theological questions. What is wisdom? Where is wisdom to be found? How is Israelite wisdom related to Egyptian and other ancient Near Eastern sapiential literature? Is Proverbs 1–9 and its explicitly theological wisdom reflective of early or late developments in Israel? These and related issues have been at the heart of biblical wisdom scholarship.[3]

In spite of the popularity of wisdom literature in recent biblical scholarship, comparatively little attention has been given to the educational agenda of the sages. While studies of the literary functions of Proverbs and holistic approaches to the book offer some help in this area,[4] there has been little attention addressing the use of this literature in ancient Israel's education and of its pertinence for contemporary education.[5]

To ask questions concerning the educational agenda of Proverbs presupposes that this literature had a pedagogical purpose and function. Though some readers and students of wisdom literature would debate such a presupposition, I assume that one possible and important use of this literature was instructional.[6] In studying Proverbs, I make a distinction between poets and teachers, between those who originally produced the aphoristic literature and those who taught its truths. This distinction between literary product and the ongoing

3. See the essays in James Crenshaw, ed., *Studies in Ancient Israelite Wisdom* (New York: KTAV Publishing House, 1976), and the bibliography cited there.

4. See, e.g., James G. Williams, *Those Who Ponder Proverbs: Aphoristic Thinking and Biblical Literature*, Bible and Literature Series 2 (Sheffield: Almond Press, 1981); and Robert Alter, *The Art of Biblical Poetry* (New York: Basic Books, 1985), 163–84.

5. See note 3 above; D. J. Estes, *Hear, My Son: Teaching and Learning in Proverbs 1–9* (Grand Rapids, Mich.: Eerdmans, 1997); C. F. Melchert, *Wise Teaching, Biblical Wisdom, and Educational Ministry* (Harrisburg, Pa.: Trinity Press International, 1998); and Walter Brueggemann, *The Creative Word* (Philadelphia: Fortress, 1982), 67–90.

6. The difficulty of dealing historically with this issue stems from the "deadening silence," ("the gulf that frequently exists between representatives of the past—often, but not always, fathers and mothers who value the tried and true—and of the future—sons and daughters whose efforts to break free from all restraints lead them to question traditional claims," *Education in Ancient Israel*, vii) which is a part of the title of Crenshaw's masterful volume on biblical education. This has led some to dismiss the instructional dimensions of wisdom literature altogether (though see notes 3 and 7 for exceptions). Again, I would propose that one way of dealing with this issue is to use contemporary theories of pedagogy in a comparative way to illuminate a difficult biblical issue, with huge implications for the present day.

process of education sometimes represents a very fine line, for surely both poets and teachers, theoretically, possessed an educational agenda. It is all too easy in focusing on the poet to slip into a search for original meaning, to try to discern what wisdom was for those who wrote it. While such study is valuable, the process by which such wisdom was taught is often ignored. A focus on those who used the poets' figure of Wisdom or creation helps us better understand the educational agenda of the wise of ancient Israel.

Raising the question of the wisdom teachers' educational agenda also raises a series of social issues. Where did these teachers teach? Who were their students? How is this teaching related to other literary traditions in Israel (e.g., Torah and the Prophets)? Examining the educational process in Proverbs will help to resolve some of these long-standing social questions about the sages and their students.[7]

One of the special characteristics of wisdom literature is its unwillingness to speak directly and explicitly of the current social problems facing particular communities. Therefore, it is difficult to reconstruct particular social settings. Nevertheless, since all scriptural communities are characterized by a dialogue between a text and the contemporary community, it is difficult to believe that such problems did not exist or that the teacher did not wish to prepare students to face them. Partially because of this character of Proverbs, my starting point in this chapter will be contemporary educational problems and contemporary notions of education and of how a teacher can and should function.[8] How can educational theorists, taking seriously the problems of our present day, help us understand the nature of Israel's wisdom literature and the teaching process reflected in it? This

---

7. See the discussion of these questions in John C. Gammie and Leo C. Perdue, eds., *The Sage in Israel and the Ancient Near East* (Winona Lake, Ind.: Eisenbrauns, 1990).

8. Though there are many possibilities to choose from, this chapter will use the writings of Donald Schon and Chris Argyris (Argyris and Schon, *Theory in Practice: Increasing Professional Effectiveness* [San Francisco: Jossey-Bass, 1982]; Schon, *The Reflective Practitioner* [New York: Basic Books, 1983]; and Schon, *Educating the Reflective Practitioner* [San Francisco: Jossey-Bass, 1987]) as the basis for comparison and contrast with the teachers of Proverbs 1–9. Argyris and Schon have not only provided provocative new educational theories, they are deeply committed to a critique of reigning models of education, thereby involving their readers in a broad discussion of pedagogy in the twentieth century. Their theories have already been used in other areas of theological education (e.g., John Cobb and Joseph Hough, *Christian Identity and Theological Education* [Chico, Calif.: Scholar's Press, 1985]; and Jackson Carroll, *Ministry as Reflective Practice: A New Look at the Professional Model* [Washington, D.C.: Alban Institute, 1986]). While Schon's writings in particular offer valuable insights for students of biblical wisdom literature, comparing and contrasting the theories of any contemporary educational theorists to the educational agenda of ancient Israel's teachers may result in significant interrelationships.

approach shapes the ancient text by reading it in light of current concerns, though it takes seriously a common educational task modern culture shares with the poets and teachers of Proverbs. However, it is true of any scriptural dialogue that the text also shapes the community, helping that community to understand its new problems in light of abiding realities that are otherwise easily forgotten. Thus, there may be insights and values in the text that are at odds with contemporary educational theory.

The Sages and Reflective Practice

The writings of Donald Schon and Chris Argyris study the nature of contemporary professional education and practice. Schon especially attacks the present goals and methods of professional education, which he believes do not accurately and adequately address the ways in which professionals should be taught or the ways in which they function in society.[9] He traces a crisis of confidence in professional knowledge, based on the application of theory to instrumental decision making, with an emphasis given to technique. Schon calls for a new epistemology of practice that views the nature and role of the professional in a different way, emphasizing artistry and competence already present in practice. What is needed, he believes, is a view of education that focuses on the teaching of a process of reflection in action.[10] Such a reflective process is characteristic of what professionals can and must continue to do in dealing with situations of uncertainty, uniqueness, or a conflict of values.[11]

Can the insights of Argyris or Schon provide a valuable perspective from which to view biblical wisdom? Clearly the process of reflective practice that Schon has located in the modern professions can be seen as a way of thinking, of viewing the world and its problems, that, when contrasted and compared with the way in which the sages as teachers use the figure of Wisdom and creation, provides us with helpful ways to understand the educational agenda of ancient wisdom teachers.[12]

---

9. See Schon, *Reflective Practitioner,* 3–20.

10. Ibid., 21–69.

11. In developing such an epistemology and setting forth possible ways in which it can be discerned and subsequently taught, Schon uses examples from many contexts to illustrate the ways in which professionals function, the kinds of questions they ask, and the educational theory that may be derived from their practice. Ultimately, an epistemology of practice motivated by a critique of current educational theory results in a wide-ranging definition of professionals and professional education.

12. See another way of addressing this problem in chapter 6.

Viewing biblical sages as reflective practitioners raises several questions about their roles as educators. First, were the sages of Proverbs reflecting on a knowing-in-action, or were they simply applying a body of knowledge for the purpose of making instrumental decisions? If the former, is the type of knowledge presupposed tacit in nature, that is, found in our action? And is one task of teachers then to find ways to make that knowledge explicit? Such knowledge will often be manifest not in theoretical propositions but in situations of uncertainty and surprise. Second, were the sages problem solvers, or were they trying to identify the problem? Do wisdom teachers frame or set problems, providing parameters and variables that must be considered if the problem is to be addressed seriously and solved?[13] Third, are the sages constructing a behavioral world, even a virtual world? Such a vision of the role of a sage would argue against the use of technique and formula as the key for learning how to live well, to have wisdom. Are the sages more concerned to provide a framework within which faithful living occurs, or to provide helpful hints on how to live such a life?

Were the wisdom teachers of Israel reflective practitioners? Both Schon and Argyris eschew the role of the professional as an expert, as the one with all the answers, with all the theory to incorporate into practical situations. Schon suggests this role is more like that of a coach attempting to teach the artistry of practice.[14] In what ways is this role analogous to that of the sage? If, for example, we were to view the figure of Wisdom in Proverbs 1 or 8 as a role model for the sage, we might see the sage as the repository of all wisdom, accompanied by a fairly rigid and hierarchical social system for teachers and students. On the other hand, if we were to dissociate the role of teacher from that of Wisdom, might it be possible to portray ancient Israelite sages engaged in educational endeavors with a role similar to that which Schon describes?

How committed were the sages to the theories of behavior and action that they taught? One mark of a good teacher, according to some, is the ability to be flexible, adaptable, and open to new questions and critical interchange of ideas while remaining committed to a particular theory of action. Studies of wisdom material suggest similar roles for the teachers of ancient Israel, albeit, perhaps, from within a certain construct of reality that the poets have drawn.

---

13. Schon, *Reflective Practitioner,* 63 and elsewhere, makes the case that setting or framing problems is a primary task for professionals.
14. See Schon, *Educating the Reflective Practitioner,* 100–118.

I have raised questions concerning the roles and tasks of the wisdom teachers with little attention to their motives. But the identification and setting of problems does suggest a possible motive: the changing of behavior. In what ways may we see wisdom teachers as those who discern dilemmas? To the extent they do this, are the sages functioning prophetically, addressing current dilemmas and calling us back to perspectives and teachings we have forgotten? Or, through their perception of the world, are they actually creating dilemmas of which we were unaware? What purpose is served by either of these actions? Are we being asked to consider new behavior? How may we learn this new behavior by listening to or reading aphoristic literature or poems about wisdom and creation? Do the sages recognize or care about learning binds that may prevent their students from entering the real or virtual world they wish to create?[15] Are the sages able to take the truths of the poets seriously but also to adapt them to new problems that at present prevent their students from understanding and appropriate behavior? Where is the community in this educational endeavor? Is there a public means of testing both the methods and goals of the teachers as well as those of their students? Do other bodies of literature in the Hebrew Bible help us to answer these questions? Finally, is competent performance or reflection upon knowing-in-action the goal of the wisdom teacher for the student? If so, who sets the values that ultimately determine the success or failure of any particular performance?

Are the answers to these questions to be found partly in the wisdom writings themselves[16] and partly in the wider public arena where other values define success quite differently?[17] The juxtaposition of contemporary educational theory with wisdom teaching has raised many significant questions for future study.

Wisdom, Creation, and the Construction of Knowing-in-Action

How can these questions we have raised about the educational agenda and methods of the sages be answered? More specifically, how might wisdom teachers in Proverbs have used the figure of Wisdom and the concept of creation?

---

15. See Schon, *Reflective Practitioner,* 125ff.
16. See Carol F. Fontaine, *Traditional Sayings in the Old Testament: A Contextual Study,* Bible and Literature Series (Sheffield: Almond Press, 1982).
17. E.g., in the areas discussed by Schon and Argyris.

The wisdom texts discussed here are illustrative. The choice of text, topic, or theme is not as important as an intentional juxtaposition of educational motives and methods, contemporary and modern. I do not wish to suggest that the poets' construction of the figure of Wisdom represents the reflective practitioner. In discussing the pedagogical uses of this literature, we are several steps removed from the poets who wrote this literature. Our question is whether creation and the figure of Wisdom in Proverbs can be conceived as a part of an educational agenda similar to that of a contemporary reflective practitioner.

> Wisdom cries out in the street;
>> in the squares she raises her voice.
> At the busiest corner she cries out;
>> at the entrance of the city gates she speaks:
> "How long, O simple ones, will you love being simple?
> How long will scoffers delight in their scoffing
>> and fools hate knowledge?
> Give heed to my reproof;
> I will pour out my thoughts to you;
>> I will make my words known to you.
> Because I have called and you refused,
>> have stretched out my hand and no one heeded,
> and because you have ignored all my counsel
>> and would have none of my reproof,
> I also will laugh at your calamity;
>> I will mock when panic strikes you,
> when panic strikes you like a storm,
>> and your calamity comes like a whirlwind,
>> when distress and anguish come upon you.
> Then they will call upon me, but I will not answer;
>> they will seek me diligently, but will not find me.
> Because they hated knowledge
>> and did not choose the fear of the LORD,
> would have none of my counsel,
>> and despised all my reproof,
> therefore they shall eat the fruit of their way
>> and be sated with their own devices.
> For waywardness kills the simple,
>> and the complacency of fools destroys them;
> but those who listen to me will be secure
>> and will live at ease, without dread of disaster." (Prov 1:20–33, NRSV)

The LORD by wisdom founded the earth;
    by understanding he established the heavens;
by his knowledge the deeps broke open,
    and the clouds drop down the dew. (Prov 3:19–20, NRSV)

The LORD created me at the beginning of his work,
    the first of his acts of long ago.
Ages ago I was set up,
    at the first, before the beginning of the earth.
When there were no depths I was brought forth,
    when there were no springs abounding with water.
Before the mountains had been shaped,
    before the hills, I was brought forth—
when he had not yet made earth and fields,
    or the world's first bits of soil.
When he established the heavens, I was there,
    when he drew a circle on the face of the deep,
when he made firm the skies above,
    when he established the fountains of the deep,
when he assigned to the sea its limit,
    so that the waters might not transgress his command,
when he marked out the foundations of the earth,
    then I was beside him, like a master worker;
and I was daily his delight,
    rejoicing before him always,
rejoicing in his inhabited world
    and delighting in the human race.

"And now, my children, listen to me:
    happy are those who keep my ways.
Hear instruction and be wise,
    and do not neglect it.
Happy is the one who listens to me,
    watching daily at my gates,
    waiting beside my doors.
For whoever finds me finds life
    and obtains favor from the LORD;
but those who miss me injure themselves;
    all who hate me love death." (Prov 8:22–36, NRSV)

In Proverbs 1 and 8 the figure of Wisdom is the speaker. Creation is an important topic in 3:19–20 and 8:22–31, but it is not necessarily related to the figure of Wisdom in the former, while it is directly related in the latter. In both chapters 1 and 8 Wisdom is calling, demanding attention to her message. Whether she appears as a prophetess (chap. 1) or a teacher (chap. 8) or as God's helper (chap. 8), humanity is clearly in need of her direction, in need of following her, understanding her, even possessing her to the extent to which this is possible. One of the problems in chapter 1 is that some, at least the simple and foolish, are not listening. For these people the message is fairly straightforward: There is a price to pay, and it appears it may be too late for the foolish. Or perhaps the point is that there will always be those who will not listen to and follow Wisdom and who will invariably pay the price. In this latter instance the audience may not be the foolish at all but those who will see in the demise of their unwise neighbors the confirmation of these sages. In chapter 8 there is a much fuller description of the message of Wisdom, providing the reasons why she is worthy of being obeyed and sought. The poem concludes with a call for obedience. In this chapter, Wisdom is to be found in all facets of the world. She is integrally related to and even responsible for all power structures of society.

In 8:22–31, Wisdom is tied to the act of creation, placing her before all else and seeing her as present during the process. The priority of Wisdom, by being there from the first, and her role as a companion are stressed. Although 3:19–20 does not refer to the figure of Wisdom directly, when juxtaposed to 8:22–31 it is not incompatible. Whether we speak of a figure (chaps. 1, 8) or something more general, wisdom is to be seen as both a critical part of what was necessary for God to create the world as well as an essential part of the finished product, built into the created order. As always, a central issue for all our texts is how searchers find wisdom in the created order. That we are called to do this seems clear in all our passages.

Wisdom and creation have several different functions in these texts. Regardless of what role or picture is assigned to her, personified Wisdom clearly raises the issue of authority. We are expected to obey her, to follow her teachings. We are to understand that she has both helped to establish the created order and will help to implement the principles and values that govern our behavior. Wisdom represents a goal to work toward (whether seen in terms of obedience or its results), something to be at least partially possessed and attained.

Wisdom also represents a process—a path, a direction, a series of values, and a priority—that must be found in our lives.

Creation is used to describe the order of the created world. It reflects the purpose and planning of God as best we are able to discern. At least in Proverbs there are similar ties and potential connections with creation passages found in Genesis.[18] This observation points to a common function shared by Torah and Proverbs: the use of a series of natural phenomena to describe both the created order and the activity of creation.

Whatever else these passages with the figure of Wisdom and creation deal with, issues of authority and order are important. One of the important characteristics of the modern professional lies in the ability to be a designer.[19] In situations of complexity and uncertainty there is often the need to impose order if we are to be able to identify the issues and arrange them so that effective action may be taken. The emphasis on creation in Proverbs provides wisdom teachers with a framework for engaging in this particular activity. The teacher might use this picture of the created order as both an example of specific tasks that must be accomplished (e.g., establishment of social, political, or religious order) as well as an affirmation that such tasks occur upon a matrix of order that is first and foremost theological in nature and origin. This latter affirmation will finally relativize all our attempts to understand and control such an order.

In constructing or imposing order, the modern professional often draws upon a repertoire of images, maxims, and values that are central to the particular field of expertise as well as to the experience of the teacher.[20] This activity seems analogous to the ways in which creation and the figure of Wisdom are described. A teacher or sage may use a wide variety of ways to set forth the content and locus of a message to a particular audience as a means of understanding the nature of particular actions and problems. In this sense, Wisdom and creation become generative metaphors used to design an order or context within which appropriate behavior may be understood to take place.[21]

If ancient wisdom teachers, like the contemporary reflective practitioners, use the figure of Wisdom and concept of creation to design

---

18. See George Landes, "Creation Tradition in Proverbs 8:22–31 and Genesis 1," in *A Light unto My Path: Old Testament Studies in Honor of Jacob M. Myers*, ed. Howard N. Bream, Ralph D. Heim, and Carey A. Moore (Philadelphia: Westminster, 1974), 279–93; and Donn F. Morgan, *Wisdom in the Old Testament Traditions* (Atlanta: John Knox, 1981), 112–14.

19. See Schon, *Reflective Practitioner*, 76–104.

20. Ibid., 60, 66, 138, 141.

21. Ibid., 269.

and impose order, they also are engaged in framing a context, setting a problem. Problem setting involves naming the issues that must be dealt with and framing the context within which the problem or issue must be addressed.[22] It seems very likely that such an activity could be compatible with the wisdom teacher's use of Wisdom and creation in Proverbs. For example, the teacher's approach to the figure of Wisdom in chapter 1 might well focus on the authority of this figure and therefore the need to discern what she is saying if we wish rewards rather than punishment. Similarly, a focus on creation in either chapter 3 or 8 sets the issue of ordering within a theological context. In both instances, Wisdom and creation do not provide answers for the teacher; rather, a context is framed and parameters set within which any issue must be discussed. In this sense, it is not the answer that the teacher is moralistic about, but rather the world within which that answer must be found, a world framed by a theological understanding of the figure of Wisdom and her role in its creation.

It is certainly appropriate to suggest that such teaching activities are compelling or convincing only to members of a community of inquiry who share the values and commitments of the teachers.[23] This has theological and social implications. Despite the worldly nature of much wisdom literature, the theological framing of this particular poetry by the writers of Proverbs would come from communities where such framing would be meaningful. And regardless of whether the wisdom teachers were allied with the establishment of their society, there are serious divisions between the foolish and the wise that have social implications for the order described.

Finally, within such a community of inquiry of the figure of Wisdom, especially in Proverbs 8, is part of a virtual world. This may reflect an interpretation by wisdom teachers for purposes very different from those of the original poet.[24] In using the created order and Wisdom to frame and to set problems and as a context for the discernment of appropriate behavior, the wisdom teacher is trying to have his cake and eat it too. On the one hand, the values associated with Wisdom and creation in the poets' texts are and must be transferable to the real world in which the teacher lives. At this level there is congruence between the poet and the teacher. At another level, however, this

---

22. Ibid., 40.
23. Ibid., 166.
24. An example is the way in which a much later picture of the figure of Wisdom, such as that found in the Wisdom of Solomon, could be placed within the Proverbs text, altering its original intention dramatically.

world in which Wisdom is found, bustling about the streets, calling to anyone who will listen, and this world in which Wisdom is an observer and helpmate in creation is a place to speak of priorities and of values safely.[25] We are even free to change aspects of this world, to reconstruct it from time to time with different parts of our repertoires, to create new metaphors. Surely this is, at one level, what Proverbs 3 and 8 represent.[26]

When our texts from Proverbs are viewed as a whole, we are left with two different pictures of creation as well as two not totally compatible pictures of the figure of Wisdom. And regardless of the poets' original intentions, subsequent wisdom teachers are now free not only to mix and match but perhaps to engage in the creation of still other virtual worlds themselves.

Problems and issues that need to be addressed in new ways in part motivate the work of contemporary educational theorists. We can also assume the teachers of ancient Israel were asked to address problems where uncertainty, conflict of values, and uniqueness occurred.[27] While the wisdom poets often affirmed the mystery of God and our inability to discern the way God acts in the world, they also demanded that we be constantly involved in that endeavor. If certain parallels may be appropriate between the teachers of wisdom and Schon's reflective practitioner, we must now briefly examine other parallels that provide at least part of the motivation to teach: to deal with dilemmas that arise in society. It is important to know not only what the teachers are doing but why. Therefore, it will be necessary to relate the wisdom teachers to the rest of the society in which they functioned and to the normative literature found within it, as well as to make some hypothetical suggestions about a historical context where this interrelationship could function.

The Sages, Torah, and the Educational Task

Through a comparison with contemporary educational theory, at least one task of the wisdom teachers of ancient Israel has been high-

---

25. "Virtual worlds are contexts for experiment within which practitioners can suspend or control some of the everyday impediments to rigorous reflection-in-action" (Schon, *Reflective Practitioner*, 162).

26. Perhaps the context of a practicum in which the teacher creates a virtual world for the purposes of reflecting on behavior is an appropriate assumption for the educational agenda and method of wisdom here.

27. See, e.g., William P. Brown, *Character in Crisis: A Fresh Approach to the Wisdom Literature of the Old Testament* (Grand Rapids, Mich.: Eerdmans, 1996).

lighted, namely, the sages' concern to provide a context for understanding the character of faithful action. The use of the figure of Wisdom and creation play significant roles in this reflective, pedagogical activity. The role of the sage highlights one essential part of what it means to be a scriptural community: the translating of the worldview and values of the text into a contemporary setting. Such an activity is related to the daily life of Israel. Indeed, the process of reflection-in-action described by Schon has some interesting and pertinent parallels with the centerpiece of scripture in the Hebrew Bible, that is, Torah.[28] Consider the following sequence:

1. The practitioner (in biblical times a member of the faith community) brings various strategies of action and understandings of particular phenomena (ways of framing problems) to any given situation. Torah may be seen to contain such strategies and understandings in the stories and laws found in Genesis through Numbers.
2. Our routine responses to new situations often result in unexpected outcomes, since the circumstances have changed. We are surprised. In Torah, the book of Deuteronomy appears to take account of such surprises, suggesting that in the new land we are about to enter, adaptations of the law to new circumstances will become necessary.
3. The new situation that challenges old values and brings new data into the picture forces us to engage in a process of reflection in action. We try to identify the new elements that have surprised us, attempting to figure out what went wrong, what will not fit. The book of Deuteronomy, the second law, reveals such a reflective process and makes the process itself paradigmatic for all future generations.[29]
4. The process of reflection-in-action questions critically all the assumptions that have been made about the previous action and theories that have been mandated. Ultimately, new ways of framing, and perhaps even new, or certainly revised, values and structures are established. Surely this is one way of understanding the law of Deuteronomy, which is new but not new, revised in light of

---

28. The structure of the reflection-in-action process used here may be found in Schon, *Educating the Reflective Practitioner,* 228–29.

29. Although such a process probably lies behind many of the different laws in Torah, it is the book of Deuteronomy that structurally performs this (canonical) function.

the new circumstances in which the Israelites will find themselves, and imbued with a humanistic frame and rationale.[30]

5. Refection finally gives way to experimentation as we seek to see if our new values and reformulation of ways to know-in-action will work. The book of Deuteronomy itself does not do this but simply mandates that we must do it as we progress, with Joshua, toward the promised land. In one sense, this activity will characterize Israel wherever she finds herself. It is surely tied to a conscious educational endeavor to attempt to bring Torah into relationship with every new circumstance in the life of the people.

It is a reasonable assumption to suppose that similar educational paradigms are functioning for the sages, the wisdom teachers of ancient Israel, and the communities that were shaped by Torah.[31] Moreover, these paradigms are compatible with the community-text dialogue we have maintained must characterize any scriptural community. While most contemporary educational theorists are not concerned with scripture, many are concerned to know how we reflect in action on the new, how we integrate that new into behavioral worlds that presently exist, and how we teach our students to do this. Torah maintains many of the same concerns, though one piece of the past that must always be a part of the dialogue is the law. As Deuteronomy demonstrates, that law may change. But what will not, indeed cannot, change is a reflection upon the written and authoritative text.

The wisdom teachers of Israel were also deeply involved in such a reflective process. While we cannot assume that the poets of Proverbs were using Torah, they were surely providing structures of authority and order that were compatible and congruent with the theological presuppositions of Torah. Issues of authority and order were also important to Torah. Perhaps more important, the setting of a non-negotiable theological context or frame to deal with these issues is also something Torah and wisdom poets and teachers share. The wisdom teachers, intentionally or not, were fulfilling the process found in Deuteronomy by reflecting critically on issues of behavior found in the poets in light of new and changing circumstances and values. Both Deuteronomy and the wisdom teachers represent an all-important, even a life-maintaining, function of a scriptural community: to trans-

---

30. See, e.g., Moshe Weinfeld, *Deuteronomy and the Deuteronomic School* (Oxford: Oxford University Press, 1972).

31. See, e.g., Ecclesiasticus and chapter 1 above.

late and to reflect critically upon the textual knowing-in-action that has been handed down to all of us. Without such a process, the text becomes stagnant and irrelevant.

What are the implications of such common functions for wisdom teachers and Torah interpreters? First, these functions suggest that any picture of ancient Israel that attempts to separate the wise from other groups within the culture is inaccurate. Second, it suggests that the educational task, as seen from the perspective of a continual and mandated process of reflection in action upon the scriptures, is central to whatever it means to continue to be Israel. The structure of Torah we have described is in all probability postexilic in origin, and therefore we should not assume a parallel role for the sage-teacher prior to this. Moreover, it has often been noted that the sage became increasingly influential as an interpreter of scripture in the post-Ezra communities of Israel. Torah is the center of the scripture. Scripture and its interpretation became a central part of the postexilic community. The sages became more involved and familiar with Torah.

One of the central tasks of the communities of postexilic Israel was to make sense of Torah and other authoritative literature in light of the many dilemmas that affected them. In light of the parallels between Torah and the educational agenda of the wisdom teachers, it is perhaps more easily understood why the rabbinic sages ultimately became interpreters of Torah par excellence. The history of such a development is still shrouded with uncertainty,[32] but the role of postexilic wisdom teachers provides one clue to unlocking the mysteries of such a process, which finally resulted in talmudic Judaism.

Future Directions

I began with the assumption that contemporary society and wisdom literature shared a common concern, namely, education. Focusing on the teachers who used Proverbs, I have asked what issues or questions about these teachers might be raised by juxtaposing contemporary educational theories and insights to Proverbs. We have discovered that contemporary theories about reflective practice can be utilized to understand the roles and functions of wisdom teachers.

---

32. Cf. chapter 1.

But an important question still remains unanswered. Is this study merely an example of our ability to find anything in a text and then, perhaps, to draw on the authority of the manipulated text to justify our results and to provide a rationale for our own twenty-first-century educational agenda? On the one hand, we have certainly seen how contemporary concerns may be used to understand a text by creating a way to view and interpret it in light of present issues, theories, and problems. On the other hand, the theological framing of questions concerning authority and order would appear to be a firm and unchangeable perspective that the text imposes upon our contemporary educational agenda. But other issues need to be identified that may reflect places where the text refuses to bend to our method.

We have distinguished between the teacher of Proverbs and the poets who composed this material. How fair have we been to the poets? Should we look for other educational models and contexts that will be more faithful to the ways in which wisdom poets wished to communicate their message? Central to our assumptions is a claim that one way to view ancient wisdom teachers is as reflective practitioners who intended to draw us into a process of reflective inquiry. Is this the intention of the poets who composed Proverbs? What other intentions might the text have? Instead of providing a context for such inquiry, does the text intend to proclaim a fairly rigid system of values, a hierarchical theological and social system that is meant to answer our questions definitively rather than to suggest the framework within which they will be addressed? Is the figure of Wisdom to be viewed as the giver of values rather than to be used as a part of a virtual world in which those values need to be located, discussed, and even changed? In other words, are these values already established and fixed, or are they open to debate?

A tentative answer to these questions is both positive and negative. When we look at Proverbs 1:20–33, it is certainly legitimate to posit that wisdom is reflective of a rigid system that cannot be changed. According to this poet, those who are foolish will perish. Those who are wise will flourish. But even assuming that we are absolutely certain of what constitutes foolish action and what does not, Proverbs 8 suggests there is still time to change behavior, still time for the foolish to turn around. When all of Proverbs is taken into account, there is flexibility to the call and demand of the figure of Wisdom. This suggests the teacher is free to debate and ponder what is truly wise and what is not, who will perish and who may still have time to change this behavior.

On the other hand, the role of creation in Proverbs is much less flexible. The often dimly perceived order of our world is theological in origin and nature. If we are to search for glimpses of that order, if we are to understand the rationale behind it, we must locate it with God and with Wisdom, who was there at the beginning.

Much remains to be done. Examining the educational tasks of ancient Israel's wisdom teachers with the help of current educational theorists must be done in tandem with scholarship that focuses on the poets who composed these texts. Such scholarship forces us to take these texts and their intentions seriously as we attempt to understand how they may be used to address the critical educational issues of our time. It helps us to understand how free we are as teachers to adapt and debate the values of the texts.

We must also continue to place our constructions of ancient sages and their educational agenda into sociological and historical contexts. Are the functions of these sages, as identified by comparisons with contemporary theories, compatible with what little we know of education and teaching in Israel? In all probability we will not be able to construct specific educational settings (e.g., the school) as a result of our research. But perhaps by understanding a bit more of the educational agendas of wisdom teachers we will be able to relate different parts of the Hebrew Bible to each other more convincingly. In doing so, we may better understand the developments in Israelite religion that led to changing roles for the sage and other literature in Judaism and Christianity.

Finally, because the issue of how we engage in education in our religious communities and contemporary society is not simply a question of what the texts and poets meant, perhaps the present approach to biblical wisdom will result in new insights for our current tasks. How could we use biblical wisdom literature in a practicum situation? How can the framing of practice viewed from a biblical perspective inform contemporary decision-making processes? Do the wisdom teachers of old have anything to contribute to the erasure of the learning bind that presently confronts us? Surely some dialogue with the new, while still maintaining a theological frame for all our investigations into wisdom, will be a part of the answer into which we must live.

CHAPTER 4

Behavioral Goals and Political Issues
The Sages and Hope

Another facet of the sage's life is the concept of hope and its implications for contemporary living. Hope for the sages may be best viewed as a process rather than a result. Though sages are often seen as advocates of the status quo, the establishment, or the institution, their hope is in a process of behavior that does not guarantee prosperity, longevity, and status but does promise at least a glimpse of wisdom.

The word *sage* evokes many different associations and meanings. In this chapter, primary attention will be given to the wisdom literature of the Hebrew Bible (Proverbs, Job, Ecclesiastes, and a few psalms usually associated with the sapiential traditions of ancient Israel). While the definition and the social location of the sages in ancient Israel continues to be debated, there is little or no debate that the wisdom literature of the Old Testament was produced by sages, however defined.[1]

A scholar characterized wisdom literature in this way: "It is the sort of literature that more often than not seeks to persuade by causing the audience to think, rather than simply demanding assent to its

---

This chapter was first presented at an international conference on hope at Chinese University, Hong Kong, in November 1996, sponsored by the religion department of Chung Chi College, Chinese University, and the Graduate Theological Union (Berkeley, California).

1. Cf., e.g., John C. Gammie and Leo C. Perdue, eds., *The Sage in Israel and the Ancient Near East* (Winona Lake, Ind.: Eisenbrauns, 1990).

world-view."[2] This observation may be helpful in exploring the way hope is to be understood in wisdom literature. We often associate the sages with institutions, with the status quo, with the establishment. Such an understanding of the sages might lead one to think of their hope as an institutional vision or a specific reward for life lived well and wisely. However, the sages can also challenge us to think, and that process of thinking and living is a way of orienting ourselves toward wisdom. What if that process were the substance of our hope rather than the institutional garb in which it is cloaked? To put it another way, though the institutional source or locus of wisdom and sages may change, the orientation toward and commitment to searching for wisdom, wherever it is found, does not change, and in it there is hope.

After examining the rhetoric of hope in Hebrew wisdom literature in a brief and necessarily illustrative way, I will ask some questions about hope and its significance for the sages in the biblical period. These questions will provide the basis for discussion and conversation that will include a much larger number of sages in other religious traditions.

There are, indeed, a number of interesting parallels or points apparently held in common between the sages of ancient Israel and the sages of China. In the early periods of Israel's history, sages were close to invisible, with the exception of the literature with which they are associated and the figure of the wise king, the paradigm of sages, Solomon. In later times, the sage became increasingly associated with the function of the scribe and with the transmission and interpretation of the sacred writings.[3] Sages were seen as conservators, as the authors of practical wisdom, who gave their students advice on how to live skillfully and well. From time to time, certain sages (e.g., Solomon and Confucius) became so wise that one can begin to speak of sages as social constructs rather than normal flesh-and-blood people—despite the very earthy wisdom associated with them.[4] Whatever is or is not to be made from parallels in China to these Israelite phenomena and others,[5] it is worth asking whether the way in

---

2. Ben Witherington, *Jesus the Sage: The Pilgrimage of Wisdom* (Edinburgh: T&T Clark, 1994), 3.

3. See chapter 1.

4. See chapter 2.

5. See Julia Chang, *Confucianism and Christianity: A Comparative Study* (Tokyo: Kodansha International, 1977); John B. Henderson, *Scripture, Canon, and Commentary: A Comparison of Confucian and Western Exegesis* (Princeton, N.J.: Princeton University Press, 1991); and the many writings of W. T. DeBary.

which hope is used by the sages of ancient Israel rings common bells in Chinese religious traditions. Most important, perhaps, is the question of whether or not hope as understood by the sages has anything to say to persons living in the early twenty-first century.

The Vocabulary of Hope in Hebrew Wisdom Literature

There are three major roots in biblical Hebrew that are used verbally and nominally to speak of hope.[6] These roots contain the element of waiting, of expectation, as a part of their meaning. The most frequent appearances of verbs and nouns associated with these roots and dealing with hope occur in the wisdom literature.[7] We expect prophets to speak of hope, and they do. We expect priests and pray-ers to speak of hope, and they do. But of what significance is the fact that the sages speak of hope more than anyone else?

One other interesting observation is that the Psalms and the prophetic literature contain far more of the verbal uses of *hope*.[8] This leads to another question. If the sages are conservative, that is, if they are conservators and apologists for established institutions, should we not expect their hope to be an object, something static, affirming the status quo? And if this is the case, is not a use of the noun for *hope* more congruent with such a perspective? The wisdom writers are far more concerned with process when they speak of hope, while the prophets may, in Witherington's words, be closer to seeing hope as assent to a particular worldview.

Textual Examples

Proverbs 24:13–14. "My son, eat honey, for it is good, and the drippings of the honeycomb are sweet to your taste. Know that wisdom is such to your soul; if you find it, there will be a future, and your hope will not be cut off" (RSV). First things first. For all sages in ancient Israel,

---

6. *kwh* (with the common noun *tikwah*), *bth*, and *yhl*.

7. That is, 32 percent of all such occurrences are in the wisdom literature. The Prophets contain 27 percent, and the Psalms contain 28 percent. If wisdom psalms (including Ps 119) were to be included with wisdom literature instead of Psalms, the proportions would reflect even more of an imbalance for the wisdom literature.

8. The Psalms contain 39 percent, the Prophets 35 percent, and wisdom literature 16 percent (though if Ps 119 is added to wisdom the percentages change dramatically). The wisdom literature dominates the use of the noun (66 percent; Prophets, 16 percent; Psalms, 11 percent).

hope is associated in one way or another with wisdom and with the search for it. There is, and perhaps will always be, a debate about what wisdom is in ancient Israel and how one will recognize it when one sees it. But there is no debate about the need to have wisdom as one's priority and guide. This passage is not at all clear about what the hope of the seeker after wisdom will be. Many commentators suggest that it is probably a combination of things we normally associate with the good life: wealth, health, success, status, and longevity. Perhaps, but what is clear is that hope is associated with the process of searching for and finding wisdom, whatever wisdom is and wherever it is found. Even Qoheleth, who had grave doubts that such a process would actually lead to wisdom,[9] still believed that this is the best game in town, especially when one is young.

Job 4:6. "Is not your fear of God your confidence, and the integrity of your ways your hope?" (RSV). This question of Eliphaz to Job is, of course, loaded. On the basis of what we know of God and Job to this point in the book, we cannot agree with the answer presupposed by this rhetorical question. In the end, however, the book of Job as a whole will affirm the truth of this rhetorical question and will restore and reward Job precisely because of the integrity of his ways, albeit with a few reprimands. There is then a fundamental affirmation about hope to be found in this text: that keeping faithfully to the path or way of the wise or righteous or pious is the basis for hope, regardless of the circumstances in which the person is found. Being fair to the etymology of the term for hope *(tikwah)* means that we must recognize the future-oriented nature of this term and therefore the possibility that it contains success, status, and similar rewards sometime in the future. But for the moment, this text suggests that hope, the looking forward to an uncertain but promised future, is justified and grounded by integrity.

Job 13:15. "Behold he will slay me; I have no hope (or "Though he slay me, yet will I trust him" [KJV]); yet I will defend my ways to his face" (RSV). My high school Bible teacher taught me the now out of vogue translation from the King James Version as a wonderful example of Job's faith and piety. As I have gotten older, the version that sees no hope against God has often made better sense of my experience. But both versions have validity and represent ancient readings of a difficult text. Most important for our purposes, the interpretive options within the ancient Hebrew do not affect the definition of hope, simply whether it is a positive or negative factor in Job's thinking.

---

9. See, e.g., Eccl 8:16–17.

To understand hope in this passage, we must pay attention to the latter half of the verse: "I will defend my ways to his face." Regardless of whether Job is a trusting soul in the presence of a killer, or whether he knows all is lost, he will defend and explain his ways to God. Given the judgment upon Job and the reading of 4:6 above, it seems legitimate to see here in chapter 13 an example of Job's integrity, of his keeping to the path he believes must be taken. Perhaps there is an irony in the critically accepted reading of the Hebrew text where hope seems to be negated, for the substance of what hope means for Job is epitomized in his actions and response.

Psalm 119:114. "You are my hiding place and my shield; I hope in your word" (NRSV).[10] This text is not from the wisdom literature in the Hebrew Bible but is usually associated with both scribes and sages. At one level, we could interpret this verse as a narrow and rigid view of both God and the biblical tradition, one in which the sage/scribe/believer clings for dear life. It is possible, however, to interpret this verse in light of the way in which hope has been used and seen by earlier sages, for this psalm text is the latest of the texts we have examined. Viewed in this manner, the verse does not necessarily emphasize the narrowness of God's word or the hope of the meditator, but instead clearly defines the locus and perhaps the guidelines drawn from the "word." For this psalmist, hope cannot be separated from the "word." So the integrity of Job's ways and the hope of the authors of Proverbs are, for the psalmist, to be related to God's word.

In this psalm we witness a transformation in process. This transformation is further explicated and developed by Ben Sira, leading to a time when the sage will be associated with the interpretation of the Hebrew Bible in general and Torah in particular. This will be a time when whatever hope there is for the future of God's people must have a biblical (textual) component and, usually, a sage as its articulator. With such a development, we leave the Hebrew Bible and its sages, moving to the time of the rabbis.[11]

Proposals, Questions, and Possible Connections

To pay attention to the presence and distribution of hope language in the Hebrew Bible is to conclude that the sages, the authors of wis-

---

10. See also verse 81: "My soul languishes for your salvation; I hope in your word."

11. "Word" is one of many references in this psalm to Torah. See chapter 1 for a discussion of the development that led to such an affirmation by the sages and scribes.

dom literature, are, relative to others within their societies and times, advocators of hope. Exactly what the sages hope for is not clear in the passages that use this terminology. We can say that the hope of the sages will often result in material wealth, in success and all its trappings. More importantly, we can usually associate the teachings of the sages with some institution (e.g., family, monarchy, school) in ancient Israel and with concerns to keep the status quo. With King Solomon as the sage par excellence in ancient Israel, this is hardly a surprising observation.

To ask another question, "What is the basis of the sage's hope?" casts a different perspective on this concept and its meaning. Here wisdom and our search for it must be central components of hope. While there continues to be discussion about what wisdom was and is, and about where it is to be found, the mandate to seek it is clear. There is a way to walk in this world that may lead to wisdom, and that way is always wiser than its alternatives. This observation, precisely because it has been formed and shaped in the crucible of human experience, affirms and identifies the sage's hope, regardless of the particular institution that may ultimately help to make this hope become a more substantive reality.

Where do the values and guidelines necessary for walking the path in integrity come from? How are we to orient ourselves to the world of institutions and other claimants on our loyalty and our faithfulness? Given their Torah-centered piety, the later sages of Israel had an easier time answering this question. The earlier and usually anonymous sages who wrote the biblical wisdom literature lift up for us humanitarian values and speak of a creation-based universalism as the context for living such values out. Here, it seems, might be one place where Asian and ancient Hebrew sapiential traditions could share their visions and hopes for humankind and the societies in which wisdom is found without encroaching on each other's particularities.

Unlike the prophets, the sages of ancient Israel do not speak of hope in conjunction with the coming of God to build or rebuild a particular people. Rather, beginning with a firm belief that the ability to search for and discern wisdom has been given to all human beings, the sages of ancient Israel speak of hope primarily in terms of the human behavior congruent with such a search. If we search for wisdom, then we have hope. If we think we are searching for wisdom but really are not, then we delude ourselves and there is no hope. The basis for our hope, for our knowledge of wisdom, is grounded in human experience, in the created order, and is manifested more often than not in human institutions such as the monarchy, the family, and the court. But, as Job, Proverbs, and Qoheleth all demonstrate, hope is finally the walking of the path, not the rewards given along the way. Without this focus on process, the sage's hope is misunderstood. The sage does not hope for a monarchy, or a family, or a state. Rather, those things are usually, but not always, given to the seeker after wisdom, but they are never the substance of the hope, merely its context.

Contemporary Hope and Wisdom?

In what sense do the sages themselves represent a hope? By whom and for whom are the sages a hope? Consider three contemporary examples where sages and hope might be pertinent. In the fall of 1996, Hong Kong was involved in a search for a chief executive who would lead the new Special Administrative Region into the future. It was interesting to see the different people who vied for this position and the public's response to them. Many argued against having a businessperson, since they believed this constituted one of Hong Kong's weaknesses, namely, too much attention to business and not enough to social services. Others argued that some of the intellectual candidates were too far removed from reality to be able to be the politician called for. One thing was clear: If the present head of the civil service had been willing to run, she would have had a great deal of support from the public, more than anyone else. Is not such a person, whatever her personality and her charm, closest to the noble man ideal of Confucius, the skilled servant of the government? The sages might have a closer counterpart in the intellectuals who put themselves forward as candidates, but the people would rather have others lead them. One also wonders whether Confucius, with his concern for governmental social service, for example, would be satisfied with the people's final hope and judgment. Of course, the governmental authorities chose the businessman, symbolic of an economic basis for power in contemporary Hong Kong and China.

It is always intriguing to examine the utopian politics of the Chinese Communist Party (or at least its public communications' face), with its focus on the "building of a spiritual civilisation"[12] in China. The emphasis on morality, on placing the president of China in the company of Sun Yat-sen, Mao Zedong, and Deng Xiaoping has often been in the headlines in Hong Kong. This is reminiscent of the

---

12. Quoted from the *South China Morning Post*, 7 October 1996.

building of sages such as Solomon and Confucius, which created a picture much larger and more authoritative than life.[13] How this applies to the current call for a more spiritual and moral civilization in China I am not sure. How much hope is engendered by such developments? But they do seem to share much with the wisdom of sages past, Hebrew and Chinese.

Finally, consider the figures of George W. Bush and Bill Clinton in the United States. Both are associated with serious commitments to the political arena, though one (Bush) comes primarily from a business background. One is characterized by vision and intellect (if not wisdom), the other with a call for a new leadership, a moral leadership. Together these very different figures have much that most societies hope for in leadership, much of it compatible with the wisdom of both Asia and the Bible. But rarely does one person have all this wisdom. Rarely is one person capable of engendering unqualified hope in the future of the state, and this is surely true at this time in the history of the United States. Perhaps we are left with the hope of the sages, but not built upon the finite and fallible people or institutions of society, though surely taking them and their abilities seriously. Rather, our hope is in the process of working toward the composite wisdom of both a George Bush and a Bill Clinton; recognizing our ability to get there is graceful indeed.

---

13. See chapter 2 for a discussion of this phenomenon.

II.
LOCATING
CONTEMPORARY SAGES

Sages and the University
Is There Wisdom in Higher Education?

This chapter places the sages of the Bible and their writings into dialogue with the modern university and higher education. There has been a great deal of discussion recently about the modern university and its relationship to classical education.[1] In addition, there is an ongoing debate about the place of theology and religious studies in the university.[2] In light of these discussions and debates, how can the ancient sages and what they cared about contribute to our understanding of the goals and purpose of contemporary education in the modern university?

A primary purpose of this chapter is to locate some of those who function as sages in contemporary society.[3] Are sages to be found in the university? If so, what do they do and where exactly are they found? Is searching for wisdom a goal of higher education? Where might we find such activity? Does it permeate the entire curriculum of a liberal arts school, or is it to be found only in certain

---

1. Cf. Allan Bloom, *The Closing of the American Mind: How Higher Education Has Failed Democracy and Impoverished the Souls of Today's Students* (New York: Simon & Schuster, 1987); and Martha Nussbaum, *Cultivating Humanity: A Classical Defense of Reform in Liberal Education* (Cambridge: Harvard University Press, 1997).

2. Cf., e.g., W. Clark Gilpin, *A Preface to Theology* (Chicago: University of Chicago Press, 1996).

3. Surely the university is not the only, or even the primary, place where wisdom is sought in contemporary society. For another far-ranging search, see Tony Schwartz, *What Really Matters, Searching for Wisdom in America* (New York: Bantam, 1995), and the discussion in the conclusion to this volume.

places? If the latter, are such activities optional for students, or are they not?

To answer these questions we will need to search for the seeker of wisdom, the sage. We must determine if there is compatibility and continuity with ancient sages who cared about living well, who focused on rationality, on breadth, on experience, and on certain systems that helped to place experience into a perspective that could be learned and then applied to contemporary life. Does the university care about any of this? In engaging these questions we will look at the goals, the history, the curriculum, the relationship of theology and truth, and, as just one example, the present concern with diversity in higher education. We must always keep in mind the nature of the university as an institution and its relationship to the broader community, that is, the culture and society of which it is a part.

Are Sages Found in a University?

A special problem arises when we attempt to determine the relationship between ancient sages of Israel and the university. The university has a long and rich history, and its mission, purpose, and pedagogy have changed dramatically over the centuries. Moreover, the university is surely not a monochromatic or monolithic institution in any society. There are many different universities, and they possess different missions, philosophies of education, and organizational models. But all universities are educational institutions. It is here precisely that a problem arises, for we know little or nothing about schools of any kind in Israel until late in the postexilic period. To ask, then, how the sages relate to a later educational institution like the university when we have no analogue or potential parallel in ancient Israel is a challenging endeavor. I will begin by focusing on what we know of the sages in wisdom literature, without specific mention of schools, and then determine whether contemporary parallels may be found in the modern university setting. Perhaps there are sages today fulfilling similar functions, who understand their roles and functions in the same way as sages of old.

At first glance, there seem to be many parallels between the goals of the university and those of ancient biblical sages. Both are in one sense derivative, for their value is seen in light of a community or society or culture that authorizes and validates their work. Sages and universities need communities to fulfill their missions and are logically subsequent to these communities that create and call them into being.

Ancient sages and universities exist to serve society, providing educational opportunities necessary for the maintenance and sustenance of these societies. Both sages and universities are involved in searches for truth and wisdom, endeavors that require certain priorities and reflect a particular series of values. Moreover, knowledge is one of the results of university education and of being a sage. Sages and universities are both concerned with behavior, with providing values and guidelines for responsible and good living within their respective communities and societies.

In light of these parallels, we might well expect to find contemporary counterparts to the sages in the modern university, notwithstanding the lacunae in our knowledge of schools in biblical times. But if we are to find sages today, more study and comparative work of both universities and the sages will be necessary. The modern university is heir to two quite different models of education that bring with them different methods of pedagogy.[4] *Paideia* describes a classical model of education that focuses on (1) a master teacher (sage?), (2) certain normative and prescribed texts to study, and (3) a goal of formation for citizenship and responsibility within the society.[5] *Wissenschaft*, at the heart of the development of the modern university in Europe, refers to a different way of carrying out education. Focused on critical research, on praxis, and on skills, the teacher works together with the student on common research and study, with the goal of achieving competence in a particular field and, therefore, contributing to society in this special area.[6] The sage has often been associated with *paideia*, though this concept is not often at the center of the university's educational mission or pedagogy. Nevertheless, John Henry Newman has argued powerfully for such a classical view of the university, and clearly there are some characteristics of this pedagogical and educational concept still functioning today.[7] At the same time, viewing the sage as a practitioner and as one researcher among many is a bit different slant on the ancient figure.[8] Though the university and sage possess many common goals, the educational philosophies and

---

4. See, e.g., the two works of David Kelsey, *To Understand God Truly: What's Theological about a Theological School* (Louisville, Ky.: Westminster/John Knox, 1992), and *Between Athens and Berlin: The Theological Education Debate* (Grand Rapids, Mich.: Eerdmans, 1993).

5. See the classic treatment by Werner Jaeger, *Paideia: The Ideals of Greek Culture*, 3 vols., trans. G. Highet (New York: Oxford University Press, 1965).

6. See Kelsey, *To Understand God Truly*, 78–100.

7. See F. M. Turner, ed., *The Idea of a University* (New Haven, Conn.: Yale University Press, 1996); and Nussbaum, *Cultivating Humanity*.

8. See discussion in this volume, pp. 69–74, 85–100.

pedagogical traditions of the school are mixed. It is still an open question whether the teachings and roles of ancient sages are compatible with the goals and pedagogy of the modern university. What is the purpose of this higher education? How might that purpose be related to the agendas and concerns of the ancient biblical sages? For John Henry Newman, the goal of university education was to produce a gentleman.[9] Much ink has been spilled in observing that the early twenty-first century is not able or ready to accept Newman's goals, even if they were made more inclusive. The focus on a classical curriculum and such a seemingly impractical goal are not capable of being sustained by many universities today, for economic as much as philosophical reasons.[10]

In the United States of the mid-nineteenth century, roughly the time when Newman was writing and delivering his lectures on the nature of the university, an educational development was taking place that "insisted that the survival and prosperity of a republic depended on educated citizens and on leaders, especially members of the learned professions, who brought religiously informed culture to an expanding nation."[11] This goal seems quite compatible with the *Wissenschaft* type of education that was reigning in Germany at the time. Professionals are looked to as leaders, as conveyors of values to the culture at large. Would these professionals eventually become modern sages?[12]

Martha Nussbaum has recently argued for a liberal education with the goal of producing responsible citizens.[13] Nussbaum defines citizenship and its attendant characteristics in light of classical philosophy and ancient Greece. Though she argues strongly for diversity within university education, she also suggests that this is not incompatible with liberal education in its best, classical, sense. To a certain extent, Nussbaum is offering a revisionist rereading of classical education *(paideia?)* that incorporates contemporary concerns and developments but is still grounded in values and goals stemming from very ancient times. We will need to explore whether or not a sage

---

9. See, e.g., F. M. Turner, "Reading *The Idea of a University*," in Turner, ed., *The Idea of a University*, xv, and elsewhere. Surely the ancient sage would be capable of affirming Newman's ideals for a university, including the focus on universal learning across a wide group of fields.

10. Cf. the essays discussing Newman and his work in the context of the contemporary university in Turner, ed., *Idea of a University,* 255–361.

11. Gilpin, *Preface to Theology,* 47.

12. See chapters 6 and 7.

13. See, e.g., Nussbaum, *Cultivating Humanity,* 294.

could function in such a modern educational environment. We have seen, however, that such a combination of new and old is basic to understanding the identity and primary concerns of the sages.[14]

The Curriculum: Is Wisdom Sought, or Taught, at a University?

The university lives with a tension between the practical (utilitarian) and the impractical. What is the use of this education? In what tangible and clear ways will we benefit from this experience and use what we are learning? What is the application to which this education is directed? Being a good citizen or a gentleman or a good thinker or prepared in some general way to deal with life's challenges have not always been adequate goals of education or a sufficient answer to these questions. To get a good education is often seen to include preparation to do something very specific, something that will earn money and provide a way of living in some specific occupation. Surely there are many professional and technical schools that have such practical goals, but the university has always had a larger vision, one that did not reject the utilitarian but saw other goals as important, even more important, before focusing more narrowly to learn a profession or occupation.[15]

What might the ancient sages contribute to our understanding of this long-standing issue? The sages, as the university, would be divided on this issue. On the one hand, the sages emphasize how to live well. On the other hand, the sages also focus on rationality, on using one's head, developing the powers of observation and analysis to construct systems of understanding. Here the sages seem to finish on what is seen as the nonutilitarian side of the debate. The sages believe that developing the ability to ascertain the established order of the universe is most important educationally. While the practical benefits of such an ability will be to live well, little or no attention is given to the type of instruction or training that will be necessary to accomplish this, or to particular occupations that might enable this to happen.[16] Where then might we find such a sage in the university today? Will it be in the practical disciplines or the professional schools?

---

14. See, e.g., pp. 5–14 above, and pp. 140–43 below .
15. See Newman's debate with John Locke on this topic, Discourse VII, "Knowledge Viewed in Relation to Professional Skill," in Turner, ed., *Idea of a University*, 108–26.
16. See chapter 7.

The modern university is moving away from the classics, away from the canons of any given field in times past, toward more diversity and less concern with the mastering of a set body of knowledge, literary or otherwise. While some see this as a lamentable development in contemporary education, it is hard to find a judgment against it in the sages of ancient Israel. It is not clear at all that there was a canon or series of classics or any set of fixed texts or other things that all students searching for wisdom might be expected to study. There were surely perspectives and systems to be exposed to, but how and when are very unclear to us. By the time of Ben Sira, we may surely argue that the wise would know the story of Israel and the fundamental values proclaimed by the evolving scriptures, but more than this we simply do not know. The biblical sages were important in the development that leads to the central place of the Bible and its authorized commentary as canon for the community of faith.[17] Subsequent systems of education will depend on the sages for transmission, expansion, and interpretive oversight of the integrity of this canon.

The modern university does not focus on behavioral goals or on the instillation of particular values, though both behavioral patterns and lifelong values are shaped and nurtured in this context. With the exception of schools with an explicit and usually confessional religious affiliation, however, the behavioral patterns and values are associated with particular professions and less with the general education that comprises much of the liberal education found within the university. Universities often contain many professional schools, each espousing different values and evaluations of society. The university does not usually choose one pattern or norm; rather, it relates all of them to a search for truth that is multifaceted, even if at times appearing to be filled with contradictions.

Searching for God, Wisdom, and Truth at a University: A Possibility?

The growth of the modern university, dependent upon events and movements within and contingent upon the Renaissance, Reformation, and Enlightenment, was not inseparably associated with theology. This is not to deny the association of theology and the university, to their mutual benefit and misfortune, from an early period. It is simply to affirm that each of these entities possessed con-

---

17. Cf. chapter 1.

stituencies that were not always identical and that did not force association for the mutual benefit of both.

Indeed, from the perspective of the university, an association with theology was often seen to represent a return to dogmatism and control by the Church, something the Enlightenment and historical-critically informed members of the university community were loath to accept. From theology's perspective, the university sometimes represented an arena with secular disciplines, which no longer used or wished the legitimation of the Church for their methods and results. The traditional domination of the university by the Church on the one hand, and the continuing need for university-educated clergy as a primary constituency of the university on the other hand, did nothing to calm the waters of this relationship.

The intertwined history of theology and higher education witnesses to some fundamental commonness while also reflecting some significant differences. We cannot ignore the institutional communities and conflict between Church and state, Church and university (private or state). The question before us is whether or not sages, shaped and formed by traditions and values similar to those of the biblical period, are capable of functioning as teachers, researchers, and leaders in the contemporary university. Part of the answer to this question depends not only upon long-standing debates between theology and the sciences through the Church and the university but also on the nature of the ancient sage. Suppose, for example, that the ancient sage is not really outdated in terms of pedagogy, education, and wisdom.[18] Then it is possible that the model of sage in a contemporary university, shaped by ancient models, may shed some light on long-standing debates and questions.

In very different times, John Henry Newman and Martha Nussbaum have argued for a conception of liberal education based on models and paradigms found in ancient Greece, arguing that classical sources and values should still inform our notion of higher education and its contribution to society. The goals of higher education are quite different for Newman and Nussbaum, reflective of their historical and cultural differences. But no one would accuse either of these scholars of ignorance, of being uninformed of the current issues that beset educational institutions in their time. Furthermore, both of them argue strongly for a classical liberal education, albeit changed by the particular needs and circumstances of the day.

---

18. Cf. chapters 3 and 7.

Newman argues for a conservative or traditional vision, while Nussbaum uses her knowledge of classical philosophy to set forth a liberal vision of education in the late twentieth and early twenty-first centuries.

The studies of Nussbaum and Newman reflect a type of education that may be suited to the sage. The developing of the ability to think well, to evaluate lived experience, and to deal with contemporary issues in a way that seeks to understand what is new and not new are goals compatible with the sages of Israel.

But what is the role of religion in the university? Both Nussbaum and Newman argue strongly for the value of such a perspective, though Nussbaum is more critical and certainly does not represent a particular confessional tradition in the way that Newman did. We must remember, however, how little evidence we have for the wise being members of the established religious life of their time. Yes, some of them composed psalms and prayers, but the literature they produced does not make reference to sacred traditions or rituals or other cultic things.[19] Moreover, while some of the wisdom literature speaks explicitly of God, much of it does not. And until we come to Ben Sira's time, we have no sapiential material that deals explicitly with the story of ancient Israel, suggesting that knowing this story has something to do with wisdom. What does all this mean? It certainly suggests that ancient sages would not necessarily have been advocates for an explicit religious or theological content in courses, nor would they have argued for the need for religious schools at all.

The sages of old were rationalists at one level and firmly believed in belief structures based on an order they most often identified with a creator God, at once the giver of reason and the source of much mystery. Yet they were not confessional in their approach to the God-given order of this world and might well have been comfortable with other perspectives, as long as order was presupposed and experience, deeply reflected upon, was a part of the position taken.

Were the sages rigid? Surely some of the biblical wisdom literature itself, particularly the book of Job, would agree with this assessment. Were the sages too conservative? The textual evidence is ambivalent, ranging from an affirmative Job to a very negative Proverbs. Like Newman, the sages of old would probably now be labeled as conser-

---

19. See Leo Perdue, *Wisdom and Cult*, SBL Dissertation Series 30 (Missoula, Mont.: Scholars Press, 1977).

vatives and their vision of education seen as dated. On the other hand, like Nussbaum, the sages held fast to the values of rationality and the asking of hard questions, which prepare one to live successfully and well in this life. In the context of a professionally oriented modern university with a focus on *Wissenschaft*, surely such a position might be seen as a minority voice. But can it survive? Should it survive? And where should it survive?

Diversity: Modern Wisdom at the University?

The modern university is often challenged to incorporate new perspectives, to study in-depth some of the new fields (e.g., women's studies and African American studies). Some of this challenge is met with conservative reactions, and well it should be. Faculties are by nature conservative bodies, for they are asked to preserve and transmit a received body of knowledge and wisdom to a future generation. On the other hand, wisdom is not a static concept, and we are constantly being confronted with possibilities for new areas of study, new methods or perspectives, new individuals or groups to be involved and included. The university must be a place where dialogue occurs between old and new. There needs to be some willingness to change, if only slowly, in the institution's values and its organizational infrastructure.

Most of the time the sages will be conservators of the institution, not spokespersons for the new, the strange, and the different. They will be the ones who recognize a threat to existing systems, while, at the best of times, remembering the essentially mysterious way in which wisdom is known and made manifest.

Martha Nussbaum is clearly an eloquent speaker for the new in the contemporary university curriculum, but she is also filled with knowledge of the old, which she uses to provide an understanding of the institution and its purposes. Is she a contemporary sage? Many might say so, but from a biblical perspective she probably would not fit the bill (and not only because she is a woman). Rather, the sages of Israel were not, with the notable exception of Solomon, the leaders of the day, leaders who argued for change, even if well versed in the past traditions. The sage is the conservator, the one who might be convinced but who must challenge the proponent of change and the new. A sage, such as Martha Nussbaum, when we find one, is what we might call a prophetic sage, and they are few and far between.

The Sage and the University

How, finally, are we to relate the ancient sage of Israel to the modern university of the early twenty-first century? How does the wisdom of the Bible help us to understand and evaluate the university better? What is common? What is not? What difference does it make?

Both the university and the biblical sage are involved in transcendent activities; the search for truth and the search for wisdom, regardless of their differences, both witness to such an endeavor. Truth and wisdom are to be searched for, used as goals to work toward, embraced when found. But they are also recognized as entities never fully achieved, possessed, or understood, always standing apart from our endeavors, never equated with them. Perhaps the most significant difference between truth and wisdom is the practicality associated with the latter, with its need to result in better ways to live. Of course, a search for such wisdom does not necessarily result in success and wealth and health, though most every seeker hopes for this. But it does give understanding and an improved ability to maneuver a way through life filled with purpose in some sort of synch with the order of the world. That such wisdom is compatible with the truth sought for by the university seems clear enough, for understanding is surely a by-product of both searches. Indeed, the education that occurs at a university seems finally to have a purpose very compatible with the fruits of wisdom, of skillful living in this world. What the sage searches for and encourages us to do, as followers and as seekers, is compatible with the university's hopes for an informed and increased ability (1) to understand the world we live in and the purposes for which we exist, and (2) to live more fully in accord with those purposes, in ways responsible to social structures that influence us.

If, then, there is some commonness about ultimate purposes and goals, we may certainly also see commonness in the missions of the sage and the university. While we have little or no knowledge of biblical schools, the modern university—conceived by many as an institution for preparing young people to think better (use of the mind and, often, as with classical education, the body as well) and for preparing better citizens for our societies—may surely be a place where sages should be operative. With a close observation of the way the world is, with an omnivorous appetite for exploration of every topic and every field, with attention to the morality of behavioral patterns and options and recognition of the transcendent nature of the wisdom we seek, the sage can make a positive contribution to the overall educational mission of the university.

What are the implications of such common searches for wisdom and truth? Given the similarities, we should be loath to abandon some of the pedagogical methods often associated with the sages and their educational endeavors. Assuming parallels between ancient biblical sages and the purposes, goals, and mission of contemporary education as found in the modern university, we should pay attention to the traditional ways of teaching wisdom. Such an agenda motivates Newman, Nussbaum, and many others who believe we cannot and will not find wisdom in our time without paying strong attention to the past.[20]

Where then might we expect to find sages in the university? We might first expect to find them wherever pedagogical methods compatible with classical *(paideia)* searches for wisdom are found. The writings of Donald Schon and others are helpful in this regard, for they encourage thinking of the professional as an artist in many of the utilitarian, technical, and rational educational endeavors of the university.[21] The methods and contexts of such endeavors often look much more like the sage of classical times than the contemporary technical researcher of later times. Here pedagogy cuts across the disciplines, encouraging us, perhaps mandating us, to find sages, or to create the opportunity for developing them and their methods, throughout the university and not simply or primarily in one or another academic field. The ability to make connections and the actual, explicit making of them are two quite different things; however, the sage needs to be able to do the latter, to relate the study of physics or Homer or geology to the goals of wisdom. There is no field, religious or not, that cannot have a sage as teacher, though we may or may not find them more frequently in one area or another.

One potential benefit of the use of ancient sages, their goals, their wisdom, and their methods, is that the sages of old may be able to provide a more holistic model for understanding our world. The dichotomy between theory and praxis, so prevalent in *Wissenschaft* types of education, is yet one more polarity that may be better understood and dealt with by focusing on wisdom rather than

---

20. Such an understanding would have more than pedagogical implications (such as master teacher experiences modeled on *paideia*); it would have curricular impact as well (focus on history and the humanities, universal education, etc.).

21. Cf. chapter 3.

knowledge as the goal of education, with the sage rather than the rational technocrat as the teacher.

To relate the sage and the world of wisdom to the modern university is in one sense simply to look at the roots of higher education and to plead for a remembering, and sometimes a returning, to the ways and goals of the sage. Often in biblical times, a calling to remember and to return was a prophetic message. Here, perhaps ironically, the call is from the sage, pleading us to remember, promising us life and understanding in the world we have been given.

CHAPTER 6

Religious Educators
Professionals or Sages?

Is religious education a profession? In answering this question, a host of other questions immediately arises. For example, How does religious education compare and relate to other professions? What is the best model for the teacher of religious education: sage or professional?[1] This last question may not seem an obvious one, but it reflects issues and concerns central to religious educators as they address their roles and identities as professionals.

In a recent article, W. O. Lee and Peter T. M. Ng suggest that religious education has begun a process that will lead to "professionalization,"[2] and they discuss some of the issues involved in trying to answer questions concerning professional identity for religious educators in Hong

---

This article was written in Hong Kong in the spring of 1993 and clearly responds to issues raised at that time and place. It was subsequently published in the *Hong Kong Journal of Religious Education* 5 (1993): 151–62, and is used here with permission. I have modified it, but the basic arguments remain the same.

1. Please relate this study to the discussion of sage and professional in chapter 7, where a more general comparison is made. This chapter focuses on a particular setting (Hong Kong) as one example of a place where sages and professions are related. This chapter also tries to provide a historical overview of sages, professions, and their educational goals. This is a complement to the comparative comments made in chapter 7.

2. The definition of Dino M. Chincotta seems appropriate here: "Professionalization may be viewed as a process through which an occupation achieves the status of profession." This is from his essay, "Professionalization and Education: An Introduction," in *Professionalization and Education*, ed. D. M. Chincotta (Hong Kong: Faculty of Education, University of Hong Kong, 1992), iv.

Kong.[3] This process has resulted in increased recognition by the public and especially the government. Looking seriously and analytically at the nature of religious education and its professional characteristics (ideals of service and accountability) as well as broadening the scope and goals of religious education are all a part of this process. Moreover, this development is associated with a professional ideology, that of quality, according to Lee and Ng.[4]

All of this reflects much concern with what Chris Argyris and Donald Schon have called the professional paradigm. Professions have ideologies, ethics, arts, or techniques associated with a particular praxis, some type of organization or guild, a definable relationship to the public, some special institutional locus, and a conception of the world in which their particular activities fit and contribute to its well-being.[5] Religious educators in Hong Kong are drawing attention to those aspects of this paradigm they already have in place and are setting forth plans for achieving more fully and effectively some of the others.

There is apparently still a ways to go. Religious educators in Hong Kong want more attention given to their professional field. Though quality is the primary ideology that governs the desire for professional recognition and standing, power and status are at issue here as well.[6] Lee and Ng conclude by observing that religious educators "have made explicit efforts to professionalize themselves, and they should at least be viewed as the profession in the making."[7]

All of these developments in the life of religious education in Hong Kong are related to larger questions and concerns dealing with the nature of professions and professionalism. And, as in other parts of the world, so also in Hong Kong, there is the perennial question of whether teaching, in any context, religious or not, is really a profession at all.[8]

It would appear that the answer to our initial question—Is religious education a profession?—is multifaceted in its complexity and is in the

---

3. W. O. Lee and Peter T. M. Ng, "The Professionalization of Religious Education in Hong Kong," in Chincotta, ed., *Professionalization and Education*, 68–93.

4. Ibid., 80.

5. Chris Argyris and Donald Schon, *Theory in Practice: Increasing Professional Effectiveness* (San Francisco: Jossey-Bass, 1982), 146–47; and chapter 7 in this volume.

6. Lee and Ng argue for an ideology of quality, but they recognize this cannot be separated from other ideologies associated with being a professional ("Professionalization of Religious Education," 80).

7. Ibid., 81.

8. See the entire volume of Chincotta, ed., *Professionalization and Education* for a good review and discussion of these concerns.

process of being answered in Hong Kong. It might even be said that there is an identity question involved in the professionalization of religious education. That is, in seeking to achieve recognition and more status in the public sector, in broadening the scope of what religious education is and for whom it is pertinent, and in intentionally trying to become a profession and therefore related in some sense to medicine, law, and other professions, religious educators are defining themselves.

To the extent that this process is incomplete, it may be appropriate to suggest that the question of identity is still being worked on and answered for religious educators. Religious education has a very special place in the history of the professions, and it has an equally important place in the history of education. The intertwining and intersecting of those histories has helped to define what religious education and professions have been up to the present day. As religious educators in Hong Kong and all over the world seek to understand themselves more fully today, an understanding of their special and particular past may help both to define what they have been and are, as well as to help to determine what they can and should become. While the particularity of Hong Kong in the early twenty-first century is the stimulus, context, and a critical factor for identifying the nature of religious education, perhaps these few observations concerning the history out of which religious education comes can help guide or direct it, or at least clarify some significant parts of its identity and role.[9]

From Priest to Engineer: The History of Professions

Although the early history of professions is not very well known, it is usually affirmed that its origins are to be found in the religious establishment, more particularly, the Church. Many point to the etymology of the term *profession* and observe that the act of professing a faith is central to its original meaning. For example, Parker Palmer remarks:

---

9. By "religious education" in Hong Kong I refer primarily to the teaching of religion and the involvement of religious institutions in the public school system. This represents a quite different phenomenon from, for example, religious education in the United States. In Hong Kong, the teaching of religious education in the public school system occurs outside the boundaries of the institutional Church. Moreover, religious education teachers are not trained in Church-affiliated institutions of theological education but rather in public universities that provide very different courses of study and degrees or certificates in the field of education.

Though the history of religion and education discussed below is pertinent to all forms of religious education, the focus of this chapter is Hong Kong. The histories presented here must be adapted and assimilated to particular contexts.

Religious professional is a redundancy. A professional, as I understand it, is supposed to profess, to testify, to bear witness to some sort of faith or confidence or point of view. Traditionally, at least, it was only because he did so that he merited being called professional. I would argue that in the traditional view, a professional was religious by definition, at least in the weaker sense of the word *religious.*[10]

Because the meaning of the term *profession* or *professional* has religious roots, the earliest professionals are often identified with the clergy of medieval Europe. The priest, functioning within the religious establishment, had religious authority and a guild of brother priests, and he functioned as judge, healer, teacher, and minister. Soon, however, the professions began to be associated with secular occupations and in doing so began a process of differentiating themselves from each other and from nonprofessional occupations. Medicine, law, education, and, later on, other fields associated with special skills and trades such as architecture and engineering, became professions. Though each profession has its own history and particular development and chronology, eventually professions became more liberal and associated with society as a whole rather than simply the church or some other institution. Argyris and Schon describe this development: "The concept of the professional as guardian of the secular values of society emerged, as did the idea of professional accountability to society at large rather than to the professional guild alone."[11] Finally, the professions became obsessed by and highly associated with technique, and this in turn led to much specialization within particular professions. Today the professional is often seen as an expert in a field demanding the knowledge and use of particular techniques or applications (skills, technical knowledge) in areas that have become smaller and smaller.[12]

The professions are associated with at least two different social loci. On the one hand, whether it is a church, a school, an office, or some other place, there is an institution usually associated with the profession and with its guild. This can be a place where the activity of being professional is carried out, or a place that oversees and makes policy for professional activities carried out elsewhere, or both.

---

10. Cited in Argyris and Schon, *Theory in Practice,* 146, emphasis in original. Lee and Ng state that "studying professionalization in the context of religious education is especially meaningful in the sense that the concept of profession has a religious origin" ("Professionalization of Religious Education," 69).

11. Argyris and Schon, *Theory in Practice,* 147.

12. The history of the development of professions has been told in many ways and places. See, e.g., Argyris and Schon, *Theory in Practice,* 146–47; and Donald Schon, *The Reflective Practitioner* (New York: Basic Books, 1983), 3–76, and the bibliography cited there.

On the other hand, professions are public by their nature, responsible to a much larger social locus that is societal and cultural in character. The present activities and developments associated with the professionalization of religious education in Hong Kong appropriately reflect a concern with both of these loci.

The specialization that has characterized the well-established professions such as medicine and law has tended to atomize the fields of practicing professionals into very discrete and often seemingly arcane areas of expertise. When this happens, a legitimate question is raised as to whether the profession as a whole, in all its small and sometimes autonomous parts, is capable of being responsive and responsible to the public at large. Can all of these specialists be value carriers for society as a whole? Such questions are often raised by the guild as well as by the government and society. This concern is often couched in attacks on technique, which is sometimes seen as detrimental to the notion of professionalism and incongruent with its historical roots. As we shall see, religious education may have a very special role to play in addressing this serious critique of the professions.

Though religious education has an important part in the beginnings of the professional movement, it is also obvious, if Lee and Ng are correct, that this particular subfield of education at large has fallen by the wayside and is not yet a full profession. In other words, though religious education has an important historical role in the understanding of profession, in one sense this history is, to date, one of failure, or at least incompleteness. In some ways, religious education just does not fit with either the established Church or secular education and their respective notions of profession and professional. Why? We have seen that from the beginning, profession in the Church has been associated first with the priest, with the ordained leader. At first that leader was responsible for teaching and for most of the religious education that went on in the Church and in the public sphere as well.[13] When education began

---

13. Within the Church and in the theological education associated with the preparation of professional clergy, the division of labor between laity and ordained has an important effect on status and education. In the contemporary period, the fact that lay leaders take over the responsibility for teaching means, as one explanation, that it is seen as unimportant by clergy who do not want to do it. Arguments are sometimes made that religious education is so important that it needs special people trained to do it, or that the reason clergy do not want to be involved in education is that the task is too hard. Regardless of these arguments, however, the following results seem to occur quite often. *Professional* is redefined in such a way that this area of clergy responsibility (i.e., teaching in educational programs) is not fundamental. Instead, professional theological education (in seminaries and other places) concentrates on other roles and tasks (e.g., counseling, preaching, social action, liturgical leadership). The result? The Church then sees religious education as only tangentially professional.

to claim a professional status, however, it did so partially by arguing, along with medicine and law, that it was a secular profession to be distinguished from the religious establishment. In Hong Kong this actually led to the clergy being viewed as inadequately trained professionals for the task of teaching in the public schools. They were subsequently replaced with nonordained teachers of religious education who had the requisite training in education. As Lee and Ng have convincingly argued, one of the biggest problems religious education has had and must continue to address is its religious nature and its relationship to the secular education of Hong Kong.[14]

This brief discussion of the history of professions and the place of religious education in it seems to be a story of promise turned into failure, at least to date. But perhaps there is more to learn or glean from this history about the special character and identity of religious education. What is it, for example, about the nature of religious education that results in criticism by others in secular education and does not allow it to quite fit in?[15] Is this something religious education should be trying to shed or change, or is it something fundamentally central to its identity? Instead of trying to be like all other professions, is this characteristic worth holding onto as an important part of religious education's self-understanding and identity? Let us turn to another history, that of education, in order to answer these questions.

From Sage to Professional: The History of Education

Long before the history of professions began,[16] teaching, inside and outside of the religious locus, was dominated by the educational phi-

---

14. Lee and Ng, "Professionalization of Religious Education," 70ff. Clearly there is a rich history of this issue in many other settings. I am aware of the ongoing debates over religious studies in university contexts in the United States, which is merely one example of this large issue.

15. D. Chincotta notes that teaching is sometimes criticized for the lack of a science of pedagogy (preface to *Professionalization and Education,* iv). Perhaps, however, it is not the lack of a science of pedagogy that is the issue for religious educators but the state of being inextricably tied to more than one.

16. The history of education is well known and has been discussed eloquently by many. Although I do not quote them, I am especially indebted to H. I. Marrou, *A History of Education in Antiquity* (Madison, Wis.: University of Wisconsin Press, 1982), and Werner Jaeger, *Paideia: The Ideals of Greek Culture,* 3 vols., trans. G. Highet (New York: Oxford University Press, 1965) for knowledge of the classical period and *paideia.* For the modern period, see Edward Farley, *Theologia: The Fragmentation and Unity of Theological Education* (Philadelphia: Fortress, 1983); and David Kelsey, *To Understand God Truly: What's Theological about a Theological School* (Louisville, Ky.: Westminster/John Knox, 1992).

losophy and pedagogy associated with *paideia.*[17] Concerned with the inculcation of virtue and with preparing young men for good citizenship, the master teacher was a central part of this educational tradition, which began in ancient Greece and has continued to influence education and pedagogy to the present day. Formation of the whole person was and continues to be an all-important goal. Teaching and the public domain are inextricably tied to the Greek model, though in some later religious forms of *paideia* the knowledge to be gained, the formation to occur, was focused inwardly on the individual rather than outwardly on society or a corporate institution.[18] So important was the notion of public and corporate to what *paideia* was about that it has often been translated "culture." Someone who was educated was cultured, that is, prepared to live in society. This cultured person was knowledgeable of and in tune with society's values, even formed by them. For Christianity and Western culture, which have inherited this pedagogical and cultural educational tradition, formation of the whole person continues to be a significant part of contemporary religious education.[19] Education and pedagogy associated with *paideia* was text-oriented, and learning the classics with the help of the master teacher was a fundamental part of the process.

The figure of the sage is very important for the education associated with *paideia.*[20] The sage functions at several different levels of understanding, with diverse social loci associated with each level. The sage can be a normal teacher, or the master teacher like Socrates who surrounds himself with students. The sage may possess special knowledge, perhaps based on long years of study and on extraordinary gifts of perception. The sage may or may not be an example of successful and skillful living to be taught. But the sage does have, as a teacher, the ability to help others make virtue their own. One does not teach virtue but must know it and be able to help others to attain or be informed by it. The sage may also be someone associated with the government such as the king, an advisor, or a petty bureaucrat. Often the goal of education is associated

17. My primary starting point in this characterization and history is Europe. Though I do not wish to equate simplistically the rich and varied history of education in Asia with that of Europe, nevertheless there are many pedagogical similarities as well as a central role for the sage/teacher in both.

18. See W. Jaeger, *Early Christianity and Greek* Paideia (Cambridge: Harvard University Press, 1961), 72.

19. See Kelsey, *To Understand God Truly,* 63–75, for a good discussion of *paideia* and its importance in early Christianity.

20. For other parts of the history and development of the sage, see chapters 1 and 5.

with gaining enough knowledge to be able to function at the governmental or state level as a soldier or scholar-advisor. At another level, however, sometimes the sage assumes a larger-than-life role. He is associated much more directly with that special knowledge called wisdom, which is necessary for everyone to obtain in order to live successfully and with understanding of the world. Such knowledge is continually sought after but rarely if ever fully obtained. For those few who have been given this knowledge, their writings and words become normative. If we would seek after and be informed by virtue, if we would understand the values of our society, we must go to Socrates, to Solomon. More often than not, such sages assume this role and function long after their death.[21] The social locus with which they are associated can vary, but it will usually be public and most often associated with social order and social control, stability, and morality. The sage is a carrier of public values, epitomizing the best way to be adult in a *paideia*-centered society.[22] The roots of this Western philosophy and pedagogy can be traced to Greece. At the same time, the tradition of sages and the nature of education associated with them is not simply or even primarily to be found in Greece, but in China and other parts of Asia that have influenced Hong Kong and its education, religious and otherwise, far more directly.

As important as *paideia* has been, however, contemporary education is partially shaped and heavily influenced by another educational philosophy, which became important in Berlin early in the nineteenth century and is sometimes referred to by the German word *Wissenschaft,* or science.[23] This educational philosophy provides the model and the values for the modern research university. The presuppositions of education in this model are quite different from *paideia.* Research is an all-important priority, with teacher and student becoming a team to accomplish common goals. This stands in contrast to the classical focus of *paideia* on the study of ancient texts

---

21. See chapter 2 for a fuller description and discussion of this process.

22. Wallace Stegner's statement is pertinent here: "Unavoidably, the qualities we call adult are on the side of 'sanity,' 'normality,' rationality, continuity, sobriety, responsibility, wisdom, conduct as opposed to mere behavior, the good of the family or group or species as distinct from the desires of the individual. It is unthinkable that we should call 'adult' anyone who is unstable, extreme, or even idiosyncratic. In its purest form, adulthood is expressed in the characters of saints, sages, and culture heroes" (Wallace Stegner, "The Writer and the Concept of Adulthood," *Daedalus* 105 [1976]: 39).

23. See above, chapter 5. *Wissenschaft* refers to more than simply the physical sciences. It epitomizes an approach to education with research at its center, regardless of the particular field involved.

to gain familiarity with and to be formed by the values contained therein, with the help of a master teacher. Although the two philosophies share certain priorities, such as an emphasis on arts and sciences, the methods of formation through study of ancient texts and formation through research (asking questions, challenging past interpretations, searching for new explanations) produce very dissimilar results and suggest different roles for teachers, for students, and for the knowledge that is finally gained.

If the sage is integrally tied to the educational ideal of the *paideia* model, the professional is the epitome of the *Wissenschaft* model of education and of the excellence it seeks to achieve. At the intersection of *paideia* and *Wissenschaft,* religious education had another critical role to play.[24] One of the scholars most influential in the shaping of the University of Berlin was the theologian Friedrich Schleiermacher. He argued strongly that ministry was, along with medicine and law, a profession. It therefore needed the same type of specialized faculty at the university. From a positive perspective, the decision on the University of Berlin's part to follow Schleiermacher has meant that the study of religion and theology has continued to be an important part of public education to the present day. Further on the positive side, this decision means that a theologian with clear religious and theological interests in education played a major role in shaping not simply ministry as a profession in a new way but all professions. The value of what happened to education in the early nineteenth century can hardly be overestimated for the history of professions. Though it has taken various amounts of time for each profession, this shift to a focus on research represented by *Wissenschaft* has provided a basis on which to build a focus on specialization and the triumph of technique, which now characterizes most fields as we have seen.[25]

On the negative side, and as referred to above, to be a member of a profession today is to fall under a large umbrella of criticisms and serious questions about competence, responsibility, and concern for constituencies, as well as educational effectiveness and sensitivity.

---

24. See Kelsey, *To Understand God Truly,* 78–100.

25. "'Professional' has increasingly come to be understood in a largely functionalist and individualistic way. A 'professional' is someone who has the specialized skills needed to meet the specific needs of his or her clients one by one. Everyone from the neurosurgeon to the hairdresser is a 'professional'" (Kelsey, *To Understand God Truly,* 94). This quote reflects not only some of the concerns of the professions noted above but also a popular trend to use the word in a more general, and unhelpful, manner.

Some have blamed this on technical rationality[26] and have pointed to a false dichotomy between theory and praxis that reigns supreme in most professions. Therefore, at many professional schools, curricular structure and other policies and programs often separate important (theory) faculty from necessary but not so important (praxis) faculty. It seems to many that technology and specialization have won the day in the professions, with disastrous results for the human values that had been associated with the *Wissenschaft* philosophy in its beginnings.[27] When these kinds of developments are described, it appears that *paideia*, however important it has been in the past, may be in eclipse. Many continue to want what *paideia* was concerned with, formation of the whole person, but are unwilling or unable to find a common meeting ground between the dominant educational philosophies still based in *Wissenschaft* and its professional products, and those of *paideia* and the sages.[28]

And where is religious education in all of this? On the one hand, the history of religious education cannot be separated from *paideia*. It has been central to teaching and learning from the very beginning of Christianity and other religious traditions up to the present day. On the other hand, religious education has not only played an important part in the history of the professions, it has also had an important role in the history of education, for the change from *paideia* to *Wissenschaft* has provided the current educational model for profes-

---

26. "According to the model of Technical Rationality—the view of professional knowledge which has most powerfully shaped both our thinking about the professions and the institutional relations of research, education, and practice—professional activity consists in instrumental problem solving made rigorous by the application of scientific theory and technique. Although all occupations are concerned, on this view, with the instrumental adjustment of means to ends, only the professions practice rigorously technical problem solving based on specialized scientific knowledge" (Schon, *Reflective Practitioner,* 22–23). Such a view should be contrasted with the popular view found in note 23 above.

27. Note the following representative critique by P. Palmer: "What these modern professionals fail to understand, of course, is the ambiguity, the tragedy, the demonic quality of the technique itself! They fail to perceive, for instance, that unadulterated technique is largely responsible for the war in Southeast Asia. . . . Technique points to the politicization of reason. Technique consists of those rational modes by which some men try to conquer others. Technique results not in debates and journals but in propaganda, in elite political policies, in war, in institutional racism, and in pervasive forms of public manipulation. Technique is the mode by which both the liberal optimists and the realistic pessimists are trying to have their way" (cited in Argyris and Schon, *Theory in Practice,* 148).

28. It is impossible to discuss this issue purely in terms of educational philosophy, for the costs of these types of education will always be a factor as well. *Paideia* and *Wissenschaft* types of education have different expectations for residence, for the amount and type of human resources, for the use of technology. All of these issues are weighed against their cost and value to the constituencies involved. For modern advocates of *paideia*-based education, see the discussion of J. H. Newman and M. Nussbaum in chapter 5.

sionals. As a result of these special historical roles and what they say about the nature of religious education, religious educators, I believe, are caught in a double bind. This bind, however, tells us precisely what is special about religious education.

One way to understand this is by appealing to the particular histories in which religious educators stand. So far they have been unwilling to give up either, but for how long and why? From the beginning, religious education has been at the heart of what *professional* means. There are many good reasons, even with all the criticisms leveled against the professions, for religious education to want to continue the developments begun in Hong Kong and to become a full-fledged and legitimate profession with all the rights, privileges, and responsibilities pertaining thereto. On the other hand, religious education has also had a long relationship with *paideia* and its philosophy of education. Must this be given up? Do religious educators have to jump from one history to the other? The educational history is the one being challenged. To give it up is to give up the sage. What is really at issue? What will be gained or lost? Is this really an either/or question? Must religious educators choose between being professionals or sages?[29]

Sages, Professionals, and Religious Educators

We must answer these questions that concern the identity and roles of religious educators raised first by the contemporary situation in Hong Kong but that are also directly related to their special place in the histories of the professions and of education. To do so we will explore the compatibility and congruence between sages and professionals in contemporary society. After this, the roles and functions of religious educators can then be compared and contrasted with those of the professional and the sage.

Could sages, wise ones such as Confucius or Solomon, be perceived to function as professionals in the modern day?[30] To be sure, sages and professionals share many common functions and concerns. Both are associated with ethics, ideologies, special worldviews,

---

29. It is important to note that *Wissenschaft* educational philosophy, so much under attack in the context of the professions today, provides an all-important function for those attempting to combine it with older *paideia* goals and methods, at least for Christians. *Wissenschaft* stresses the public dimension to education in a very explicit manner, something *paideia*, with its interior focus (despite its original public concerns), in many cases desperately needs.

30. See the full discussion of this question in chapter 7.

a particular relationship to society and to laity (i.e., nonprofessionals or nonsages). There are, at the same time, at least three fundamental differences between them. First, sages are most often associated with the educational philosophy of *paideia* and its particular pedagogical methods and concerns; the modern professional is not. Second, sages are usually not associated with the particular and technical knowledge of the professions but rather with insights and concerns and values that apply to the entire society and culture.[31] That is, the constituency of the sage is societal, and the knowledge and the values the sage speaks for are more general and pertinent to all. Third, the sage witnesses to the transcendent.[32] Sages are often like saints, bigger than life, often revered and treated almost as gods.[33] Whether we ever have the opportunity to meet a sage or not, still they function, in a *paideia* setting, to testify to the interconnection of all creation and its order. They suggest that the task of understanding is a continuing one, pointing to origins or causes that cannot be possessed but that stand over the order itself. Whether this is called heaven or God or something else, most sages in most cultures share this transcendent concern and perspective. Although professionals often seek truth and have ideologies that witness to seemingly unattainable but still worthy goals, the transcendent nature of the sages is missing. For all these reasons, it does not appear that sages can function as professionals today or that most of their values and methods can be associated with those of the professional paradigms we have examined.

Can contemporary professionals (doctors, lawyers, engineers) function as sages? At first glance, the answer to this question seems obviously No for all the reasons just given. However, another reality must be dealt with before this conclusion is drawn. Even if we accept the conclusion that sages in the ancient model are not capable of functioning as professionals today, who do function as our contemporary sages? I have asked this question in many contexts over many years,

---

31. This is, of course, theoretically true for modern professions and professionals, but we have noted that in practice this fails to be a reality.

32. A helpful discussion of this aspect of the sage, for both Western (Christian) and Asian (Confucian) traditions is found in Julia Chang, *Confucianism and Christianity: A Comparative Study* (Tokyo: Kodansha International, 1977), 79–91.

33. Note the following description of a nineteenth-century South China classroom: "Every morning when the scholar enters the room, he bows first before the tablet and then to his teacher, the former is not merely a tribute of respect, but an act of worship, which he is taught, nay, compelled to pay to Confucius" (cited by Anthony Sweeting, "Historical Perspectives: The Long March towards Teacher Professionalism in Hong Kong," in Chincotta, ed., *Professionalization and Education*, 7–8).

and it is always a difficult one for people to answer. Put another way, who are the value carriers for the church and society? Who testify to ideals of service within the state and community? If we seek a modern carrier for some of these values, professionals of every type are certainly strong candidates. In theory, part of the definition of a profession is that it carries some of society's secular values. The difference between secular and religious need not concern us here, since most of the ancient sages were deeply committed to the same types of values and looked at all of life, not simply the religious establishment, in describing what wisdom is.

The problem with seeing the professional functioning as a sage today concerns the preoccupation with technique, with specialization and the atomization of knowledge that characterize the modern professions. If professionals function as sages in contemporary society, and there is certainly evidence to suggest this has been and continues to be the case in at least some areas,[34] then we have a special problem. Who will testify and witness to values that apply to all society, to knowledge that pertains to everyone and is not the property of experts who have the right techniques and status? More important, perhaps, how is society to ensure that all of its members learn the values that undergird its existence if the carriers of those values, the teachers of those values, are found in specialized areas with highly technical knowledge? Does this not suggest a situation in which each of us will learn only small parts of societal values, perhaps in a rather random manner, and then be asked to put these parts or fragments together ourselves, without ever knowing how much of the puzzle we have been given? Such are some of the questions and challenges that confront a society that has lost its sages and depends on professionals alone to fill their shoes.[35] It may be, however, that the special character and history of religious education make it particularly well suited to address these questions and challenges and thus for religious educators to function as both professionals and sages in the modern day.

---

34. Here I continue to take seriously that the professions do have an important public function and constituency and that they are also associated with some of the basic values of society. Moreover, it is certainly common to hear doctors, lawyers, teachers, and others speak of their professional fields as essential to whatever it means to live well, to live skillfully, and therefore, with a sapiential and ancient analogue, to have wisdom. See the much fuller discussion in chapter 7.

35. Work that addresses some of these issues is being done on a number of fronts. See, for example, Edith Wyschogrod, *Saints and Postmodernism* (Chicago: University of Chicago Press, 1990), in which she argues for a hagiographic ethic in light of problems with moral theory in the postmodern age.

From the beginning of the history of professions, religious education has played an important part. This history has had its ups and downs. Moreover, there is reason and legitimacy for the continued association of religious education with the professions in light of (1) the place of religion in the history of education and (2) its special intersection with and impact upon the development of professional education and the notion of excellence as professionalism. All of the developments cited by Lee and Ng witness to a new phase in that history for religious education as a profession in Hong Kong. Perhaps the rich heritage of professional and educational history in which religious educators stand will provide motivation toward the goal of full professionalization as well as other contributions to education and Hong Kong society.

As we shift our attention back to the sage and religious education in Hong Kong in the 1990s, we must remember and take seriously the multiple social loci in which religious education functions and to which it is responsible. First, taking religious education seriously means remembering that this type of education has its origins and many of its values associated with religious institutions, though the religious education we have been describing in Hong Kong by and large does not take place within the physical confines of such institutions. Second, taking education seriously in the Hong Kong context places much of religious education in the context of the public school system, and it is therefore directly related to one of the most important social institutions of society. Third, religious education is associated with and connected to its own guild, as represented by many different organizations all over the world. Finally, religious education is clearly connected to society at large through some of its most important social institutions (e.g., family and government). These observations about the social locus of religious education differentiate it from some other professions whose constituencies are much smaller and perhaps, unlike education, based on needs that do not apply to all people at almost all times.

On the basis of the social loci where religious educators function and to which they are responsible, as well as its past association with *paideia* in both religious and secular spheres, and because the particular mix of sage and professional is truly a part of what religious education has been, we must hope that in the moves toward professionalization, religious educators will not lose their function as speakers for the sages, as well as being sages themselves. Religious educators need, in light of their social locus and their rich heritage, to witness to larger realities: society, religious establishment, culture. They need to witness and call people to a task of education that is never completed but whose values are clear, if not always affirmed by other professionals.

To stand in the educational tradition of the sage means to live in tension with the goals and ideals of the professional and contemporary society. It means, on the one hand, living between a focus on the whole person with concerns for formation, for knowledge of the transcendent, for living skillfully or well, and for having wisdom and being genuinely committed to reason, technology, and expertise, on the other. Religious educators may or may not be sages, but they are called to love teaching and to witness to order, morality, and the web of interrelationships in our world as a whole. By their placement in history (and for some, in Hong Kong), religious educators seem positioned to be able to live in this tension productively, making a special contribution to the society that the other professions alone simply cannot make.

CHAPTER 7

Biblical Sages and Modern Professionals
*Strange Bedfellows or
Variations on a Theme?*

 T his chapter seeks to place biblical wisdom into dialogue with contemporary society by searching for analogues or parallels between the sages of ancient Israel and modern professionals. Chapter 3 focused on the pedagogy of the sages, comparing it with contemporary educational theories anchored in the professions. The purpose of this present chapter is to engage in a dialogical study of the biblical sages and contemporary professionals, with a special focus on their educational roles and some of the presuppositions they make concerning their purpose and raison d'être. Biblical sages and their wisdom can be helpful in understanding contemporary professions. Conversely, contemporary thinking about professions can enhance our understanding of biblical sages and their literature.

 Are the ancient sages able to be seen as the professionals of their time? There are a few possibilities, such as treaty writers, special advisors to the king, and the like, but we simply do not have enough information to be able to make judgments here. But can the ancient sages be seen today through the lens of professional identity in a way that helps us understand them better? That is, should parallels found between contemporary professionals and biblical sages influence the way we interpret ancient sapiential material today? Can current thinking and practice associated with contemporary professions and professionals become a hermeneutical lens through which we can see the ancient sages and wisdom of the Bible? In principle, given the comparative dimensions of sociology and anthropology, to say nothing of the reliance on much more traditional biblical methods, such as form criticism, upon comparative methodology, there is precedent for using contemporary theory to try to understand sages. Such comparisons may help us understand how to interpret biblical literature in valuable ways for the contemporary community of faith. Since this is a primary reason for engaging in a dialogue between ancient wisdom and contemporary society, it seems a goal worthy of striving toward.

This chapter is illustrative and provocative, not comprehensive, in its definition and use of the contemporary professional.[1] What fruits does a comparison of professionals and sages produce? To what extent do they share a common educational agenda and similar roles in society? What is distinctive between them? Are professionals a manifestation of modern sages in our society?

Presuppositions, Definitions, and Comparisons

Contemporary biblical scholarship sees the sage in biblical Israel as important and vague at one and the same time. Is the sage to be identified with the monarchy (advisors, treaty writers, literati), with the family and village (parental analogues, folk wisdom), with the school (teachers), with the cult (psalmists, keepers and transmitters of scripture and records), or with some ill-defined intellectual tradition? Recent studies have considered all of these possibilities and more. For the purposes of this particular chapter we are concerned with the writers of wisdom literature and those charged with its teaching and transmission. Whether or not these people were known as *hakamim* (the wise) or *sopherim* (scribes) in biblical times is simply not known.[2]

Professional is a term that is subject to a great deal of debate. We define the professional as one who is a practitioner, whose work is characterized by competence, by a significant social value associated with the practice of the profession. Professionals are characterized

---

1. The understandings of Donald Schon and Chris Argyris, supplemented by the historical perspectives found in the writings of David Kelsey, form the basis for my definition of professional. See, e.g., pp. 74–79.

2. See Philip R. Davies, *Scribes and Schools: The Canonization of the Hebrew Scriptures.* Library of Ancient Israel. Louisville, Ky.: Westminster John Knox, 1998); James Crenshaw, *Education in Ancient Israel: Across the Deadening Silence* (New York: Doubleday, 1998); John C. Gammie and Leo C. Purdue, eds., *The Sage in Israel and the Ancient Near East* (Winona Lake, Ind.: Eisenbrauns, 1990); and chapter 1 in this volume.

by rationality and often possess special technical skills and abilities developed through particular training. The best classical examples of professions are theology, law, and medicine. Theology has waned in importance and prestige as a professional field, though at one time its place in the university was tied to its professional character and goals.[3] In the past century, law and medicine have grown in importance, and other professions have come to the fore.[4] Whether or not teaching is a profession is hotly debated, at least in the United States. Some argue that teachers are professionals and teaching is a profession; others do not.[5] On the other hand, there seems to be no debate that teaching is an essential function or ingredient for some professions (e.g., ordained ministry in a parish).

The focus of this chapter is on sages and professionals as functioning social entities—the roles they have in society, their worldviews and presuppositions. The dialogue between ancient wisdom and contemporary culture created here raises the issue of the nature of the relationship between wisdom and community. The sages and the wisdom they search for and teach are found in normative scripture, a community text. This wisdom is seen to be one way to live out the scriptural message to community. Whether there are parallels with the professions remains to be determined.

Relationship to Constituencies and Society
Whom do sages and professionals serve and to whom are they responsible? Professionals provide services, and they can be criticized if found insensitive, dishonest, incompetent, or out of touch. This critique may come either from the constituency served or from a guild of professionals. A guild may or may not be formed because of constituency concerns and expectations. Most professional guilds eventually have to deal with regulations and standards as a part of their constituency expectations.[6]

Ancient biblical sages were not as susceptible to critique. Many of them were dead and long since canonized (e.g., Solomon).[7] Sages were often associated with the power structures of society (e.g., monar-

---

3. See David Kelsey, *To Understand God Truly: What's Theological about a Theological School* (Louisville, Ky.: Westminster/John Knox, 1992), 78ff.; and chapter 6 in this volume.
4. There are many examples: the applied sciences (engineering, architecture), social sciences such as psychology (clinical and counseling), and social work.
5. See chapter 6 in this volume.
6. The concern with regulation is usually dealt with by larger entities as well (e.g., the state).
7. See chapter 2.

chy), where criticism was not encouraged or even tolerated. Often it was the writings of these sages that were in the public eye,[8] rather than the actions often associated with many modern professions. Sages may have been designated as such not because of training and certification but because their teachings and words reflected wise opinions and judgments. Since there were no rules or regulations concerning wisdom, it was harder to criticize the teacher and carrier of it. Pragmatically, if what was taught worked and was compatible with reigning value systems and the institutions that maintained them, then sages were in a relatively secure position.[9]

Basis of and Relationship to Authority

Professionals are recognized in practice and through credentials for their competence, technical knowledge, and their particular skills. They are usually known for their ability to deal with the real world and its problems as they are related to their particular area of knowledge and skill. The behavior of most professionals is governed by regulatory agencies.[10] The public's knowledge and affirmation of this, as well as the skills and competence usually associated with the professions, form the basis of their authority.

It is more difficult to speak of authority for the sage. The rhetoric of some sages would attribute authority and legitimation to God, who ultimately authorizes the search for wisdom and therefore also the role of the sage. More likely, however, are two other possibilities. First, since the sage is known for wise words and perhaps has demonstrated wise living through his or her own life, it is the ability to live well and to write or teach about skill in living that authorizes the sage. Second, the sage's authority is derived from the institutions central to the maintenance of order in society: the family, the state, the cult, and later the school.[11] The proximity to power (e.g., the king) provides a base of authority less formally defined and yet broader than that of the professional.

---

8. How many people had access to this literature is debated, but it was surely not a large segment of society. For a concise overview of literacy and the sages, see Davies, *Scribes and Schools,* 15–19.

9. This situation changes when wisdom is equated with Torah and the sage becomes responsible for a very different type of interpretation. See chapter 1.

10. In contemporary society the professional is increasingly liable to its constituency through the court system as well.

11. I speak here of the institutional authority of the sage, in contrast to the authority inherent in the sapiential literature. While this latter concern is important and dealt with in chapter 3 and elsewhere, it is not as important for our present purposes.

Expertise

Professionals exercise power and possess authority precisely because of an expertise they are presumed to have. This expertise has been acquired through specific, regulated training and credentialing processes, as well as significant and supervised experience in the field. Thus, the professional has knowledge of something not unique and thereby capable of being standardized. The professional has the ability to apply that knowledge to concrete problems.[12]

Is expertise an appropriate qualification for a sage? To what might it be applied? Teaching, communication, living, observation? Sages were seen as those with keen skills of observation and the ability to express themselves clearly in particular rhetorical styles and literary forms. How or if the society controlled such skills and abilities is difficult to determine. Further, it does not seem particularly important in describing the functions of the sage. Was the sage an expert in living well, or rather in the articulation of how to do so? What content do sages and professionals have control over? What was the relationship of such content to particular societal values? Wisdom is important, but it cannot be regulated and valued in the same way medicine and law might be.

Behavioral World Builders

Professionals are involved in theory building and thus in behavioral world building. Donald Schon, for example, believes that the behavioral world created by professionals is in fact an artifact of the theories actually used by practitioners in the living out of their particular responsibilities.[13]

Sages are known for many systems that are intended to control and evaluate behavior, most of them retributional and moral in character. Living well according to the will of God the creator, as reflected in the natural order and in varieties of authoritative institutions, is at the heart of the sages' message and concerns. This behavioral dimension of the sages' world-building process is more explicit than for the professional and is much broader in scope.

---

12. See Donald Schon, *The Reflective Practitioner* (New York: Basic Books, 1982), 24. A question raised by this type of expertise and training is how the professional functions in unique situations where standardized knowledge and methods are not able to function well.

13. Schon, *Reflective Practitioner*, 128ff. This practical origin and function should be contrasted with a grander scheme of behavior that has little to do with what actually happens in the professionals' lives and the society in which they function. Sometimes professionals are accused of such schemes, but Schon does not believe this has much importance for behavioral worlds actually used.

Carriers and Transmitters of Value

Both sages and modern professionals set forth values associated with their special areas of knowledge. For the professional, the values are most often associated first with the guild, though there must also be accountability to the society served by the profession. For the sage, the values are usually tied to institutions (e.g., cult, monarchy, and state) rather than to a guild or a constituency served.

Education

Professional schools provide for "the transmission to its students of the generalized and systematic knowledge that is the basis of professional performance."[14] Put simply, professions have a rigorous and well-defined educational route that must be taken by those who wish to join them. Moreover, this education is mandated and controlled by the society through accreditation and other regulatory agencies.

To discuss education and the biblical sage is to ask a number of questions. Do sages teach wisdom? What kind of setting, besides the family, should be presupposed for the passing on of proverbial wisdom? How is wisdom communicated and through what institutions? A distinction must be made between the state as a symbol of the wise ordering of the world and the state as a medium through which particular wisdom gets communicated. If an institution creates sages, what is the role of education in that creation and in the further living out of that role by the sage? Are there several different types of wisdom, depending upon the institution that needs, searches for, and uses it? What is false wisdom, and how might one differentiate between this and true wisdom?[15]

---

14. Everett Hughes, "Higher Education and the Professions," in *Content and Context: Essays on College Education*, ed. Carl Kayser (New York: McGraw-Hill, 1973), 660, cited in Schon, *Reflective Practitioner*, 358.

15. To all of these issues concerning education must be added the pedagogical issue (see chapter 3). Most professionals are dependent upon a definition of their activity and their requisite education that comes from the development of the modern university in eighteenth-century Germany. Indeed, the technical rationality Donald Schon speaks of as characterizing the goals and identity of the modern profession and its educational models is directly related to the *Wissenschaft* educational paradigm, with its focus on objectivity and collegial research. On the other hand, the sages in ancient times were associated with a model of education and culture often characterized by the Greek word *paideia*. Here the model is based on a master teacher, concerned with the learning of virtue and of formation for successful living. It is important to see the differences between these educational systems and to recognize that their methods and goals will not be harmonized easily, if at all. Cf. Kelsey, *To Know God Truly*, 85, and chapter 5 in this volume.

Sages as Professionals

As they study the modern professional, Donald Schon and Chris Argyris speak of theories of action. They make a distinction between an espoused theory of action, which is the answer to the question of how someone would or should behave under certain circumstances, and a theory in use, the way in which someone actually acts in certain circumstances. Professionals give the espoused theory of action allegiance and communicate it to others, but behaviorally, like everyone else, the professional acts in accord with a theory in use.[16] How pertinent is this for the sage? Are the sages dealing with theories in use (their own) or theories of actions (others or theirs), and is this distinction valid?

A comparison of Proverbs 2 and 7 is illustrative and instructive at this point. Proverbs 2 is a long poem that calls on the obedient son to follow wisdom and gain its many benefits. A recurrent undertone of this poem is a charge to stay away from the loose woman, who will prevent the searcher for wisdom from attaining all that is promised in the poem. Proverbs 7 has many of the same themes, but also contains within it a description of a young man being led astray by a prostitute, using the behavior itself as a model for what should not be done. When these two chapters are viewed together, it seems that wisdom writers are juxtaposing an espoused theory of action ("do not be led astray by the wayward woman" in chapter 2 and some of chapter 7) with an actual theory in use (chapter 7). This juxtaposition has many interesting and valuable pedagogical possibilities.

Schon and Argyris go further and suggest that a "theory of practice then consists of a set of interrelated theories of actions that specify for the situations of the practice the actions that will, under the relevant circumstances, yield intended consequences."[17] It seems that the sages are surely engaging in the same kind of construction of theories based on their observation of human action and their clear moral value system. This is seen in the retributional system, the so-called two-ways teaching, that the sages set forth.

Another common way of understanding the work of professionals is to speak of single-loop and double-loop learning. In single-loop learning there is a highly predictable and controllable field of con-

---

16. See Chris Argyris and Donald Schon, *Theory in Practice: Increasing Professional Effectiveness* (San Francisco: Jossey-Bass, 1982), 3–19.

17. Ibid., 6.

stancy that yields fairly uniform results. The problem with such a system is that the theory builder (the professional or the sage) becomes a prisoner of the programs and strategies built upon it. The so-called friends of Job are caricatured as such prisoners, unable to move outside the cause-effect experiential analysis of Job's condition. Double-loop learning changes the fields of constancy, opening up many different possibilities for change. While such a learning process may reflect a more realistic view of the world, it does not necessarily affirm stability and order (in the sense of something that can be predicted and described accurately), something that both professionals and sages seek, at least from time to time. To say, for example, the world is out of control, is not necessarily a good beginning gambit for a professional or sage, both of whom depend on the trust and confidence of their followers or clientele. To say that we are not in control is hardly less comforting, unless whoever is in control (God, for the sages) can be predictable and consistent, something over which there is major disagreement.[18]

It seems clear that the prophets of ancient Israel were advocates of a double-loop learning process, affirming that Yahweh was the one who changes all fields. Torah contains both single and double-loop learning processes. What about the sages? In Prov 13:1 (a: A wise son heeds a father's instruction; b: the arrogant will not listen to rebuke) we appear to have a fairly straightforward single-loop learning process in each strophe, but when a and b are put together it becomes more difficult to interpret, for who is the arrogant? Here the constancy of 13:1a is called into question, perhaps changing the character of the learning process from single to double-loop learning. An even better example is found in Prov 14:1 (a: Wise women build up their home, b: but with their own hands the foolish pull theirs down). Does this proverb reflect the way the world is on the basis of single-loop learning, that is, wise women do this and the foolish do that? Or, perhaps, the wise are affected by the foolish, and vice versa, but unpredictably? It is possible to see both single and double-loop learning in the writings of the sages.

We have alluded to the system-building activity of both the sages and professionals. It is surely possible for the sages to

---

18. See chapter 8 for examples of control systems found in leadership studies and wisdom literature. Regardless of whether it is a sage or a professional or a king or a priest "in control," this desire to have anyone in control is often a manifestation of the individual's own desire for the same. That is, if God (or some other authority) is predictable in a system I can understand, then I have some control over my environment and life.

become prisoners of their own retributional systems. Job addresses this problem directly, criticizing a rigid application of retributional theology to problems of inexplicable and apparently undeserved suffering. Thus, the wisdom corpus itself and the sages who produced it are clearly involved in vigorous discussions of single and double-loop learning, with very real human examples and observations at the heart of the debate. It has been observed that professionals tend to want to hold on to their theories in use. That is, we do not usually try to effect substantive change when dilemmas occur. We value the constancy of our theories in use and our behavioral worlds. Therefore, theories in use tend to be self-maintaining. We tend to adopt strategies to avoid perceiving the data that does not fit. The biblical sages do this in their effort to conserve the institution. This is a good example of the social function of the sage. At the same time, there is already built into the system of proverbial wisdom and its rhetoric the possibility of seeing the world in a much more complex way. In addition, there are the internal critics of the wisdom tradition, Job and Qoheleth, who vigorously and publicly challenge the reigning systems and a rigid, single-loop way of interpreting the world based upon them.

Many see the professional as a problem setter rather than a problem solver. That is, the professional does not necessarily have all the answers but is capable of letting the constituency and clientele know what the problem is and what the resources are for dealing with it. Do the sages perform this kind of function? By constructing a worldview that attributes order to a God who is in control but whose ways are not always obvious or understandable, the sages indeed contribute to the setting of a problem. There is no doubt that any given proverb can be seen as an answer to the question of why someone acts like this or something happens like that. But viewed as a totality, the wisdom of Proverbs and elsewhere witnesses to a vast number of possibilities and explanations for what is wise and good. How to live well, the goal of searching for wisdom, is not a monochromatic and univalent concept but one that depends upon many variables. When the sage begins to identity these variables and also to witness to some fairly stable assumptions (about the nature of God, humanity, some institutions), then the sage is setting rather than solving the problem of how to live well and faithfully in the world given to us.[19]

---

19. See chapter 3 above for another discussion of this phenomenon.

Finally, Argyris and Schon argue that there must be a way to test assumptions publicly. Do the sages have such a way? When we may assume a school context for the teaching and transmitting of wisdom materials—that is, from Ben Sira onward—then a case can be made for such a public process of testing. Before that time, Job and Qoheleth may represent writings that performed such a function, as they surely do now for some faith communities.

As I conclude this section, in which I have attempted to cloak the ancient sage in the garments of the modern professional, it seems appropriate to look at a contemporary paradigm of the professions to determine how well the sage fits.[20]

Transforms faith into ideology. From time to time the sages can be accused of this, especially by each other (e.g., Job), but more often than not this does not appear to characterize the sage's work.

Possesses an ethic that is binding on the practitioner. This is certainly true of the sage.

Has a set of arts or techniques. If this is the case, it probably lies in the area of literary skill and powers of observation and deduction.

Guild. Surely this is true for the late postexilic and rabbinic periods, but we simply do not know about earlier times, and an argument from silence is not a positive sign in this instance.

Special relationship to laity (that is, professional deference, authority, trust). Most of this would be supposition until the time of Ben Sira. However, whether a king, a royal advisor, or a family leader, one could suppose an authoritative relationship to others.

Institutional setting. Everything we know of sages suggests a close relationship to important social institutions.

Worldview/theory (sets forth concepts of the world in which professional practices are thought to lead to a better world as envisioned in the ideology). To the extent that we can identify sages with the actions they speak of (searching for and obtaining wisdom, living wisely and well), clearly they are associating a worldview with their actions and commending it to others. Whether one needs to see the sages actually epitomizing the actions they describe is debatable.

---

20. This paradigm is outlined in Argyris and Schon, *Theory in Practice*, 146–49.

Professionals as Sages

What do contemporary professionals look like from the perspective of the ancient sages? Let us cloak the professional in the garments of the sage and see what fits and what does not.

Relationship to Tradition: Conservatives

The primary reason why sages are usually seen as conservatives is not to be found in the content of their message but rather in the social locus of their activity, especially in the institutions of monarchy and family. When viewed from this perspective it seems clear that wisdom of the sages is intended to help conserve the traditions of the past by maintaining the present institutions with which this tradition is associated.[21] Do professionals function in this way in contemporary society? A strong case could be made for this view, since the professions are usually connected with primary institutions and values central to our broader communities and state. The professions are often associated with traditional values and goals of conserving and stabilizing. In this sense, they look very much like the sages of old, though their wisdom is of a different kind.

Status Quo Orientation

This does not refer to a static approach to life, which does not see the need for change. Rather, the ancient sage was concerned with stability of existent institutions such as the monarchy and the family. When the monarchy ceased to exist in Israel and Judah, however, other institutions, even those of foreign powers, became responsible for maintaining the fabric of society. As it was within the monarchy, the message of the sage from within these other institutions was often focused on the status quo, not wishing for a radical shift into the unknown, preferring instead the good and evil one sees to that which is uncertain.

Again, when associated with such a message, the modern professional seems quite at home. The professional depends upon a stable social system, a society functioning with some predictability. The value

---

21. Given the nature of wisdom literature, we should not expect explicit affirmation of particular institutions on a regular basis. Rather, we need to ask the question of where order will be made manifest, where a retributional system of theology lives, and who is in charge of implementing some of the truths set forth aphoristically. Here we will find a variety of institutions with values and goals very close to those set forth by the sages, and this is not serendipitous.

of the professions is precisely to help build and sustain a stable society that has various needs, from medicine to organized religion to building to therapy. Open to change and development, the professional is not a revolutionary, for stability and status quo are constituent parts of the fabric of the profession and its relationship to society.

Patriarchal and Hierarchical Systems

The histories of the ancient Near East and the post-Enlightenment West are both dominated by institutions with hierarchical organizational models, most of them based on a patriarchal system. To say this is to recognize that both sages and professionals share this way of organization and, often, the rationale behind it, a rationale that highlights the value of men and denigrates women and strangers. It would be anachronistic to ask whether or not sages of old could and would have functioned in any other kind of system. However, there is no doubt that many professions are now being challenged to think in different ways, to organize themselves differently, to educate themselves differently, to change their values. While it would be premature and naïve to assume this has occurred, many professionals view the systems of the past with disdain and are trying to move the larger profession and guild toward other ways of valuing and organizing themselves. There is nothing about the sage that assumes only one kind of system is workable and best. Sometimes, however, so sages like Confucius and Solomon might suggest, compelling and convincing reasons must be given if it is argued that a system centered on a monarch or emperor with strong repressive powers is not the best means for sustaining a society. Still, here is one place where the fabric of the ancient sage's world may or may not need to be replicated by contemporary professionals.

Secular

To speak of the ancient sage as secular is to speak anachronistically and inaccurately. But I risk this criticism because the omnibus interests and almost unquenchable curiosity of the ancient sage seems best to be contained in the word *secular,* which refers to breadth and scope. At one level, it is probable that the modern professional, whose work is often defined in terms of a movement toward increased specialization within the profession, is not reflective of the ancient sage whose scope and focus seems so much broader. At another level, however, the professional and the sage do share a focus and sphere of influence that extends far beyond organized religion or cult. It is usually agreed that most sages responsible for composing biblical wisdom literature were not priests or other officials of the cult. The scope of the sages' interests had more breadth, and this seems to be the case for modern professions and professionals also. One caveat must be made, however. That is, in the modern period we may not assume that professionals are active members of any religious community, while we usually, and safely, assume that most sages in the ancient past were.

Two-Ways, Moralistic System
The heart of the sages' teaching in ancient Israel presupposed a retributional system of right and wrong, good and bad, life and death, and any number of other polarities that revolve around clear choices and their clear consequences. The sages were advocates of a system that helps us to understand the way the world works and is organized and how we, as human beings, can navigate our way through it successfully, or not. Since much of the system rests upon theological presuppositions,[22] we dare not draw too many parallels between this system and that of the modern professional. However, as behavioral world builders, professionals are often moralistic about a particular view of the world and the place of the profession in it. Sometimes such morality rests upon a system which suggests that bad things will happen if we do not have a particular profession (e.g., medicine or law) playing this role in society. At that point there seems to be little difference between use of the systems, except for the theological grounding of the ancient sages. The professional seems at home with the moralistic nature of the sages' teaching and vision.

Nonrevelational
Both the sage and the modern professional assume that our behavior and our world will not be dramatically affected by a direct revelation of God such as that experienced by Abraham or Moses or one of the prophets. We do not often know whether sages or contemporary professionals actually believe it is possible for God to act in this way or whether God has acted this way in times past. What is important is the assumption that we will not usually learn of the way the world works through God coming in fire and cloud to speak to us. The ancient sage did believe, however, that there was a transcendent God who could

---

22. See chapters 1 and 3.

often surprise and confound.[23] The world of such a God, where we live, is finally mysterious, though we have been given the ability and the need to see some of its workings and rationale and order. The professional sometimes appears to want more predictability and control. The sages' teaching and worldview seems more compatible with the way things are (with or without a God hypothesis) than that of the professional, who often sees the world in light of social goals with no theological or transcendent perspective.

Ahistorical

The practicing professional of today has a focus on the here and now, on the issues facing society, rather than being concerned to tell the history of the guild or the field or the state. This is compatible with the ancient biblical sage who, until later times, spent little time speaking of the specifically Israelite history of which he or she was presumably a part.[24] History was not important as a rationale to explain why something was the way it was, why wise behavior consisted of this rather than that, and so on. Modern professionals are often focused on *techne*, on particular skills and methods, and such a focus is often dependent upon a worldview in which history is either downplayed or unimportant. To this extent then, many modern professions would be comfortable with the focus on the ahistorical focus of the ancient sage.

Experience

The sage's teachings depend upon experience. Experience of observation and observation of experience—both of these are important. For the biblical sage, wisdom is integrally related to having experiences in some sufficient quantity to make judgments and evaluations, and to demonstrating some skill in determining what experience is saying and in finding a way to express it well and usually succinctly.[25] Experience is also at the heart of what it means to be a good professional. The professional is not simply someone with the right kind of training, acquired skill, and learning. Rather, the professional that most people want to use is someone with experience, someone who can, on the basis of that experience, clearly determine what the issues are and what the solutions will entail. Experience is

---

23. The most dramatic example of this is in Job, but see also the many proverbial statements that lift up the mysterious ways of God.

24. See chapter 1.

25. See, e.g., Gerhard von Rad, *Wisdom in Ancient Israel* (Nashville: Abingdon, 1972), 31–32.

an absolutely critical factor in the public's belief in whether or not the professional can do his or her job well and quickly. Here the sage and professional are closely linked. The sage cannot be a sage without experience and a proven ability to interpret and express that experience well. The professional's stock in the community will not be derived from a degree attained or a school attended but on the experience he or she has had and on his or her proven ability to function well. In this sense, regardless of validating agencies and all kinds of regulations, experience is what makes a good sage and a good professional, and their constituencies seem to know this.

Order

Ancient biblical sages assumed that there was an order, however sometimes dimly perceived, that pervaded creation. Moreover, that order was at least sometimes ascertainable. Living according to that order was more likely to bring success than acting against it. As we have seen, the basis of the order was theological, and some sages were clear that recognition of this was essential ("The fear of the LORD [that is, the orderer] is the beginning of wisdom"), while others did not use a theological rationale in their writing. Most important, perhaps, the order of the universe was usually found mirrored in the social institutions the sage found constitutive for society and its ongoing stability. The modern professional would probably, with or without the theological presuppositions, be very comfortable with such a notion of order, as they are with the conservative and status quo orientation of the sages. To maintain there is an order, while at the same time being realistic about the many places in which disorder or incomprehension occurs in this world, suggests that we can find at least someplace where the order is reflected and maintained. Both sages and professionals do this, though the institutions where they find the order sometimes differ dramatically.[26]

Creation

For the ancient sage, creation is not simply or primarily a thought about how the world came to be. Rather, the concept of creation maintains the derivative nature of the world and provides an occasion for reflection on how wisdom was associated with the making of the world. Thus, creation is a notion that relativizes humanity and all that

---

26. Without such a place, such an order, the rhyme and reason and purpose for professional service is called into question.

we can perceive, while providing a chance for suggesting how God and no other used wisdom to create all that is. The modern professional may or may not make use of either of these two aspects of creation as viewed by the sage. There are any number of other more modern and perhaps more sophisticated ways of describing the derivative nature of the world and humanity and their consequences. Since a "God hypothesis" is central to creation as conceived of and described by the ancient sage, and since such a hypothesis is alive and well primarily in religious communities, the modern professional's affirmation of creation seems dependent on factors very different from those of the ancient sage.[27]

Theodicy
The problem of theodicy, the presence of evil in a world controlled by a loving and just God, is one of the issues most biblical sages had to address. If we speak of the situations that create the question— namely, unexplained suffering and natural catastrophes—then surely the question of theodicy is always with us. But the primary way in which the question of theodicy is raised is with the presupposition of a God who is operative in the world. Here is where, as with creation and several other examples above, the sage and the professional part company. Although one can assume a personal decision to have faith in a God active in the world, which would then make the issue of theodicy real, this is hardly the mandate or general operating procedure of the professional.

Canon
Finally, the biblical sages are sages because the community of faith says that they are. One example of such a decision on the part of the community of faith is the inclusion of the writings of many unknown sages in scripture.[28] This gives us an all-important starting point for speaking of wisdom and sages. There seem to be other such canons of authoritative writings in the professions. Sometimes these canons describe the hopes for the professions, or the qualifications of professionals, or the contributions of the professions to society. But that a contemporary sage is in part identified and defined by a canon, an authoritative writing for a special community of faith that is then

---

27. See the discussion under *Secular* above (pp. 95–96).
28. See chapter 2 for a discussion of how the writings of these many unknown sages are often associated with a special, almost larger-than-life, sage figure.

affirmed by the larger state, seems to represent a similar process for both sage and professional.[29]

Implications and Future Directions

Are ancient biblical sages and modern professionals strange bedfellows, or are they variations on a common theme? Perhaps it is my Anglican background with its desire for compromise and the *via media*, but it seems that the answer is both. Surely we have found many common characteristics that sages and professionals share. Both are tied deeply to institutional settings and have many concerns that stem from such connections: order, stability, status quo, and conservatism. Both sages and professionals speak with moral and normative force and with authority. They, and their literature, are convinced that their contributions to society are critical.

Having said all this, there are some fundamental differences and difficulties raised by making these comparisons. The amorphousness of the sages has, on one level, allowed us to do almost anything we wanted to do but without precision, making our conclusions in many cases very tentative. On the other hand, especially when we focus on the content of the biblical wisdom communicated by the sages, we find some very basic differences. Most important is the difference in the objects that are to be associated with the sage and professional: wisdom, on the one hand, and a service characterized by the professional's skill and expertise, on the other. The sage is involved in teaching people how to live well, while the professional may have that goal, but it is achieved through a focus more on the skills of the teacher or practitioner than on the people served. The goals of the sage are to have everyone become wise, while the goals of professionals are not to have everyone become professionals. Yet the most fundamental difference of all is the theological foundation upon which the wisdom of the sages is based. Yes, the sages may be seen to be secular in their interests and concerns, and they may not pay much attention to the revelational history of Israel and to some of the authority structures derived from it. But wisdom for the sage is still fundamentally theological in character, beginning with an assumption of creation by God and a resultant natural world order associated with God in both

---

29. There are, however, very different forms of canon (legal, medical, etc.), which are the different ways in which professionals and sages are held responsible to the guild and larger society (education, competent practice, etc.).

enlightening and mysterious ways. Our ability to know and to understand and to live well are connected to God and to God's intentions for the world. Wisdom then makes no sense without God. This is very different from the professions with their anthropocentric foci. While many functional parallels may be found, there is a basic difference between the sages and contemporary professionals.

Recognizing the difficulties of comparison and some of the areas in which there are irreconcilable incompatibilities, let us return to our comparative process and our original questions. Can the contemporary professional be seen to fulfill many of the functions of a sage in today's society? On the basis of our quick overview, the answer seems to be clearly yes. Despite differences in services rendered, in worldview, and in organization (i.e., guild), the function of the professional today is very similar to that of the sage, especially in terms of its relationship to the institutions and the culture served. Moreover, a comparison of the services and goals of the professions with that of wisdom may indeed be helpful for contemporary concerns (emphasizing mystery, transcendence, the out-of-control nature of the world, etc.). While we cannot draw the conclusion that professionals are sages, we can certainly conclude that professionals fulfill many of the roles and functions that sages of old did for their very different societies.

Much more work will need to be done in this area. There are promising parallels and nonparallels that may lead us to know more of both ancient sages and contemporary culture, something the sages would rejoice in.

CHAPTER 8

Leadership and Wisdom in a Time of Chaos
A Tale of Two Solomons

Imagine yourself in a boat in the middle of a river. The current is very strong and you are being carried away, down the river, far from shore where safety and security are to be found. What do you do? You can row toward the shore with as much energy as you can muster and hope that you are able to make it. Or you can stay on the river, navigating it and being open to whatever the river brings you.

These two options for action have their parallels in contemporary approaches to leadership. There are a great many books and theories that advocate imposing some kind of control over the circumstances that confront leaders. These books and theories offer a variety of approaches and solutions to the dilemmas facing institutions as diverse as the family and the multinational corporation. This option is analogous to trying to row to shore from the middle of the river. There are lots of ways to row, lots of methods to use, and the goals of stability and safety on that distant shore are surely important. More often than not, the river (that is, the setting in which leadership takes place) is seen as chaotic, out of control, and something that needs to be escaped or at least handled as well and prudently as possible.[1]

This paper was read at several "Business of God" luncheons in 1999 for the Church Divinity School of the Pacific. I am grateful for the feedback I received and hope that the best of it has found its way into this text.

1. See, e.g., Ronald A. Heifetz, *Leadership without Easy Answers* (Cambridge, Mass.: Belknap Press, 1994); and Warren Bennis, *On Being a Leader* (Reading, Mass.: Perseus Books, 1989).

On the other hand, some books on leadership focus less on trying to get out of the river and more on how to navigate in it, perhaps even to enjoy the river despite not knowing where one will go or how one will find the shore. Though many of the same techniques or methods for rowing are to be found in these books, the value systems are quite different, for the river is not necessarily seen as undesirable, even if the places where it leads are unknown or unclear. Indeed, some think, for a variety of reasons, the apparent chaos of the river or the institutions we serve reflects an order not yet completely understood. Staying on the river is one of the best ways we have of understanding our world and therefore being able to exercise leadership in meaningful and effective ways. Instead of trying to control the chaotic and impose our order upon it, this approach to leadership advocates a more humble and modest strategy: recognizing that the apparent chaos contains an order to which leaders must be open.[2]

The issues raised and debates enjoined in these contemporary leadership studies are finally not about what technique we should use to become effective leaders. Rather, fundamentally different world-views are clashing here. Is the world in which we are all called to be leaders without order? Is one of our tasks to try and impose an order for a world, to try to control it through whatever means we have available? Or is this world, seemingly chaotic at times, essentially a world of order over which we have little control but in which, if we recognize this fact, we may nevertheless be able to exercise effective leadership? These questions, and the worldviews presupposed by them, are critically important for all of us.[3]

Leadership and Chaos

Many leadership studies share a common starting point and premise: Things are not working as well as they could and I/we have the solution to this problem. Recently the work of Margaret Wheatley, who has a different approach, has become popular.[4] While some of what Wheatley has to say is not new, two special characteristics of her work deserve our attention. First, Wheatley argues that the out-of-controlness we

2. See, e.g., Richard Farson, *Management of the Absurd: Paradoxes in Leadership* (New York: Simon & Schuster, 1996); and Margaret Wheatley, *Leadership and the New Science* (San Francisco: Berrett-Koehler, 1994; 2d ed., 1999).

3. Wheatley, *Leadership and the New Science* (1994), 3.

4. See the many favorable reviews of her work and its use in a wide variety of educational settings.

sometimes experience—the chaos we sometimes see in our homes, in our businesses, and in our churches—may not be chaos at all. Rather, it may be merely a reflection of our inability to understand the entire picture well enough to see the order inherent in the world around us. She claims we may better understand the nature of our world and the nature of the leadership we are called to exercise by looking at new science research, especially studies of the quantum world, the world of subatomic particles.[5]

Second, instead of running from chaos, Wheatley encourages all of us to embrace it, to study it, and to find, with the help of the new science, that order and direction can be found within the chaos. To return to our original situation, viewed from Wheatley's perspective, the river is ultimately not out of control or chaotic. But we must give up our own perhaps natural desire to see it as an object to be escaped or to be shaped according to our needs. Leadership theory viewed from this perspective is contextual; it suggests that knowing your world is just as or more important than any number of techniques used to motivate those with whom you work and over whom you are given responsibility. Such an approach to leadership is open to a series of changing strategies, even to some failures or missteps along the way. For the overall goal is not to get to the shore but to navigate the river and to trust that the order inherent in the world makes the river a good place to be. Viewed from this perspective, the river allows us the ability to see and experience more of our world.

The world and the order that permeates it are clearly an important subject for leadership studies. Study of the world and its order was also important to biblical writers, especially those associated with the wisdom tradition. One of the most important leaders and wisdom teachers of the Bible was Solomon, to whom we now turn.

A Tale of Two Solomons

The Bible presents two quite different portraits of the biblical king Solomon.[6] One way of presenting these different pictures is by looking at the young king and the old king. The young king, described in

---

5. Wheatley, *Leadership and the New Science* (1999), 3–15.
6. The history of Solomon is found in 1 Kings 3–11, the wisdom of Solomon is found in Proverbs, Ecclesiastes (Qoheleth), and the Wisdom of Solomon. These portraits are created less by the life and times of Solomon and more by subsequent communities with a number of different rationales. See chapter 2 for a part of this story, and standard critical introductions and commentaries for the actual historical character of Solomon and wisdom literature.

both 1 Kings and Proverbs, was well aware of his need for expertise, for special knowledge, for wisdom, as he tried to govern and lead the people of Israel and Judah. The young king studied hard, wrote many proverbs, and was known throughout the world as a wise king, a great leader. Associated with the young Solomon were good listening skills, good and equitable judgment, power and influence, authority, a special and close relationship to God, an incredible amount of responsibility, and certain tendencies to take himself and his office too seriously. The young Solomon was also a teacher, a student of the natural order, one who often referred to the big picture seen either in terms of the cosmos, God, or both. The young Solomon also affirmed the monarchical system. He believed that right and wrong can and must be distinguished, and that as king he was a carrier of the values of his society and all of the institutions. In short, Solomon's wisdom and leadership were very much tied to the institutions of his day and reflected the status quo orientation such institutions, then and now, often display. Young Solomon was a firm believer in the institutional systems and the institutional wisdom of the day. He would probably have the confidence, and maybe even the ability, to direct his boat away from the middle of the chaotic river and onto its safe shores.[7]

We encounter the old Solomon in two different biblical books, Ecclesiastes and the Wisdom of Solomon. The Solomon in Ecclesiastes is an affirmer of the absurd who states baldly that whatever wisdom he has attained in his life is not really wisdom in the sense of full understanding. He further asserts that the search for order and structure and meaning is doomed to failure.[8] Using human experience as our yardstick and guide, there is no system of reward and punishment that can be demonstrated to work consistently. The purpose of life is far from clear, and mortality is the final injustice. A leader in such a world, the old Solomon would say, should be very pragmatic and open to the whims of God and of the universe rather than relying heavily on some clear and cogent system for guidance. When the older Solomon, in the book of Wisdom, speaks of moral values and of the retributional system, he is forced to admit that the rewards

---

7. For the wisdom of the young Solomon, see 1 Kgs 3, 4:29–34, 5:7–12, and 10:1–29, and most of the book of Proverbs.

8. "No one can find out what is happening under the sun. However much they may toil in seeking, they will not find it out; even though those who are wise claim to know, they cannot find it out" (Eccl 8:17, NRSV).

for the good and the punishments for the bad may not be found in this world but in the next.[9] This is a radical departure from the young Solomon's well-oiled and functional this-worldly system, where rewards and punishments are much more immediate.

The lives and teachings of both the young and the old Solomon reflect interaction between the king, the institutions that he led, and the God of Israel. For the young Solomon, the institution of the monarchical state was his primary focus, though he relied on God's sanction and presence to justify the king's ways in the world. For the old Solomon, God was much more a central focus of his thought. But God was far off and no longer directly involved in the world of human affairs. The old Solomon still gave a great deal of practical advice for those willing to listen to his wisdom, but the ways of God and therefore of the world were finally a mystery to him. Here the experience of the old Solomon has led to skepticism, weariness, and a profound sense of mystery mixed with some bitterness over his disillusionment and disappointment. The old Solomon would probably tell us to stay in the middle of the river. This advice would not be based on a certainty of the benefits, however, but because Solomon would have no faith in our ability to get to the shore, nor would he see any point in it.

Solomonic and Modern Leadership: Comparisons and Contrasts

Solomon and Margaret Wheatley would both affirm that there is order in this world and that leadership must take this seriously in formulating strategies and goals. However, the young Solomon stands apart by maintaining that the order of this world is readily apparent. He locates the social and political manifestation of this order in the monarchy and in his own leadership, and he is quite willing to impose order on others. For the older Solomon, the order of the world is not as easily discerned, and it surely is not necessarily found in societal structures. Both he and Wheatley would argue against trying to impose an order onto the world. They would understand leadership as having an important role in helping others to seek and find an order already present in the world, albeit in incomplete ways. They would also advocate that leaders look at the big picture, the whole, when

---

9. See Wis 4:16ff., where the righteous who have died will be rewarded in eternity, not in the here and now.

formulating actions and directions, even if they recognize that whole to be more than we can ever finally understand.

The study of new science for Wheatley represents openness to new understandings and new data, which she sees as important for leadership. This is compatible with Solomonic wisdom, especially with the younger Solomon, who was much taken with the encyclopedic study of nature and the created order. The older Solomon was less flexible and less open to all this new study, having seen enough of the world, having read enough books to wonder whether any new explanation could make a significant difference in our understanding of the world and how we should live in it.

On a related topic, Wheatley and the younger Solomon might agree that information is the lifeblood of the organization. The more information and data provided, the more the leader and the institution are able to make intelligent and informed decisions, though Wheatley also sees information as that which can make systems fall out of balance, searching for order, never satisfied with the old, constantly creating the new.[10] Surely the young Solomon, always searching for new knowledge, might affirm some of Wheatley's concerns for new information while being somewhat frightened about the potential disruption or questioning of the status quo that such information inevitably causes. While the older Solomon would not be threatened by such information, he might well question its value. He would wonder whether the inevitable changes brought about through the advent of new information actually represent progress and fuller understanding, or whether they represent a circular process with many variations on a theme.[11]

Both Solomon (young and old) and Margaret Wheatley would affirm the importance of the leader as a carrier and a proclaimer of the core values of the institution, whether this be church, business, school, or family. This role forces the leader to understand and study the world of the institution from a holistic perspective. At the same time, for Wheatley, the leader is not the one who imposes a particular system, in the sense of a technical solution, on the institution as the way of understanding its nature and goals. One of the shortcomings of such solutions is their inability to provide for creative responses to the new, their inability or unwillingness to stay on the river. Here again, the wisdom of the Solomons differ. The younger Solomon is

---

10. Wheatley, *Leadership and the New Science* (1999), 96–97.

11. "What has been is what will be, and what has been done is what will be done; there is nothing new under the sun" (Eccl 1:9, NRSV).

much more interested in being a carrier of institutional values than the older Solomon, who at the end of his life is uncertain about the role of the monarchy as an institution. At the same time, the younger Solomon is, against the advice of Wheatley, more prone to imposing control systems upon the monarchy and the state. Wheatley and the older Solomon, for very different reasons, do not believe that control systems are finally efficacious.

Finally, Wheatley and the old Solomon would agree that the leader today must be deeply involved in articulating the mission of the institution. Regardless of the apparent chaos in which we live, faithfulness to the overall purpose of the institution is expected of its leaders. Such faithfulness does not demand a homogeneous or monolithic response by others in the institution, but it may indeed free them to fulfill their own responsibilities in different ways. All kings, all leaders, are subject to the temptation to identify their own interests (in power, influence, wealth) with the institution, to its detriment, but the older Solomon appears, through experience, to have grown out of this tendency.

Leadership in a Time of Chaos

How do the Bible and the contemporary studies of leadership that focus on chaos theory and the new science help us today? Many leaders and theorizers about leadership are teachers. One of their primary functions as teachers is to present the issue or challenge to the institution boldly and clearly. Such an approach helps to create institutional thinking and action, providing new thoughts and ideas. Though Solomon and Wheatley have different motives and agendas for their teaching, their pedagogical writings have this common effect.

Another element Solomon and Wheatley share is reliance upon trust. For the young Solomon, such trust is tied to the belief in his ability to control the monarchy and the state through his actions. The older Solomon and Wheatley know better than this, but still believe that trust is an important stance for the leader, even if outcomes and process are far from clear. For them, trust is located in the midst of the world, in the process of living, in the middle of the river.

Such observations bring us back to the basic biblical conversation between the leader, the institution or organization, and the transcendent, whether this be seen as the never-ending source of the new, or science, or God. Wheatley, as reflected in her basic trust of chaos and her belief that such chaos is finally well ordered, maintains a healthy interrelationship between the unknown, the organization, and herself.

The older Solomon comes closest to such a conversation, but finally does not see the possibility of a significant interrelationship between God, the organization, or himself. God is simply too transcendent to make much of a difference. Following such a model for leadership will create special problems when the new is confronted and experienced. The young Solomon is much more likely to find room for the new in his leadership, though he will always be tempted to try and control it rather than to be open to change. The young Solomon, perhaps for narcissistic reasons, is much more prone to let God be in relationship with himself as king than directly with the institution and others (hence, a problem with prophets and the cult). Without full communication between the institution and God, the young Solomon risks much, even the future stability of the state.

As we began this study, we might have expected to see more parallels and places of congruence between the older, wiser Solomon and Wheatley. Solomon has a healthy disrespect for systems and a bias against the possibility of achieving full knowledge of how things work and why. As is so often the case, the Bible surprises us, for there is much more similarity and congruity between Wheatley and the young Solomon than might be expected. Yes, the younger Solomon is much more prone to systems as the answer to how to be an effective leader and is also more likely to suggest a yes/no, good/bad solution to a complex problem, none of which Wheatley would advocate. On the other hand, the young Solomon is an active student of the world and of the cosmos, eager for knowledge and information, searching for a better grasp of the order he believes is there. But both Wheatley and the young Solomon have much to learn from the old king. We may or may not be ready to accept Ecclesiastes' final belief that wisdom is not fully attainable or even understandable, or that the world is ultimately mysterious. Nevertheless, we can benefit from the older Solomon's view of the whole and empathize with his affirmation of the apparent senselessness of it all, at least from time to time.

What is the final biblical word on Margaret Wheatley and works like hers? The Bible, at least the wisdom traditions associated with Solomon within it, wants to affirm her perspective on leadership, on the need for leaders to understand the inherent order within an apparently chaotic world while still affirming that leaders are very much not in control of these processes. At the same time, the Bible, and the young Solomon in particular, want to argue for the value of systems that have the apparent and at least partial purpose of control and of making meaning, even if they do not finally control or explain fully.

The biblical traditions would maintain that such systems of explanation were never intended to provide definitive answers. Sometimes Solomon and other leaders hold on to these systems a bit too tightly, treating them as answers rather than as directions, or partial explanations, or as a context within which answers might be provided. When this happens, it is often best to reject the systems altogether. For then, instead of being a helpful tool, they prevent an ongoing dialogue with the new, with the transcendent.[12]

Both the Bible and Wheatley would agree that wisdom is a primary component of effective leadership. Searching for wisdom can be partially achieved by looking at "how to" or system books, those which would help us to learn to row better and stronger when we need to make it to the river's edge. Searching for wisdom is also to be achieved by staying in the river, in the apparent chaos itself, and trying to navigate within it, trusting that your welfare and your institution's future will be richer for being open to the new and the order we cannot yet see. But wisdom itself is found neither in the chaos of the river nor in the "how to row" manuals. Wisdom is found in the dialogue between leader, river, manuals, and the bringer of the new, the creator of chaos and of order.

---

12. We have the ability to elevate leaders to such a level, preventing dialogue between the new and the vision of leader as infallible, all-wise, and all-knowing. We can also do this with the Bible and with several other entities. The challenge is to be open to the new while still taking seriously the past and what it has to say to us, and vice versa: being open to the old while still taking the new seriously.

III.
IDENTIFYING BIBLICAL
AND CONTEMPORARY SAGES:
Education and Wisdom
in Religious Communities

Education and the Church
A Biblical Perspective

There is a growing discontentment with the quality of education possessed by recent graduates across a wide spectrum of professional schools. As one bishop recently asked a body of seminary presidents, "Why aren't you sending us graduates who can read and write?" Though the phenomenon suggested by this question might be exaggerated, it is certainly not unique to any particular profession. Indeed, schools all over the country try to deal with deficiencies in basic skills through many different remedial programs. The significance of this phenomenon for our present study is the widespread issue it highlights not only for the church but for everyone in contemporary American society: the crisis of education.

Chapters 9, 10, and 11 were first composed as lectures in the Bible in the Church series and entitled "Wisdom and Education: Biblical and Modern" at Christ Church Cathedral, Indianapolis, 1990. Though they have been extensively reworked, these chapters still retain their focus on the contemporary faith community, its educational mission, and the role of wisdom literature and biblical sages in dealing with this mission issue. In many ways, these chapters represent one possible direction in which contemporary faith communities might go as a result of the types of study found in chapters 1–8. Because of this, despite some repetition and general introductory comments about wisdom, I have chosen to place these chapters at the end of this study rather than at the beginning. As I have stated elsewhere, however, it is the contemporary issues of the faith community that motivate these chapters. This is where we often begin, as well as end, our biblical studies.

The Shape and Contours of the Educational Crisis in American Society

Contemporary educational administrators and theorists participate frequently in conferences or other special meetings in order to deal with one aspect or another of the current state of education. When viewed as a whole, these gatherings, though usually focused on one particular aspect of education, provide a powerful witness to the scope of the problems facing the United States in this area. Whether we speak of kindergarten or law schools, there are concerns about adequate resources, finances, credibility, and related issues. Among the most frequently cited problems is our inability to keep up with other countries who have more effective and advanced educational systems. We are unable to provide enough interested and qualified students to meet the needs of many crucial professions. We do not have the financial resources necessary to sustain educational programs in many different fields and at many different levels. And, critical to all educational endeavors, there continues to be little interest in teaching as a profession. The reasons for this are clear enough: not enough financial reward, or security in some cases; the difficulty of teaching poorly motivated students; inadequate physical resources; and so forth.

The results of such problems are clear enough; in fact, they provide the primary motivation for many of the aforementioned conferences held all over the country. Secondary education is of such an uneven quality that many parents with the resources simply opt out of public education and send their children to private schools. In many cases, a good education can be had in public schools only by the specially gifted and highly motivated, leaving most students at the mercy of an inadequate system. Little wonder, then, that even if they graduate from public high school, many of these students are not "turned on" to education and the opportunities it might offer.

Many major universities have courses in remedial English that are required of all those who cannot pass a basic proficiency test. In times past, good universities simply did not admit students with such deficiencies. Now, however, the number of high school graduates who need remedial English is so great that public universities have little or no choice but to admit many of them. Clearly there are implications for the quality and shape of an undergraduate education when course time must be spent dealing with skills that should have been learned previously. And, though we can point to high school or earlier levels as critically important, the effect is snowballing, touching every place where education occurs. So, for example, we find law school graduates who need remedial writing courses, or doctoral graduates in some disciplines (often the physical sciences) who are unable to express themselves in written discourse. Where this problem begins is often subject to debate. That it affects all levels and aspects of the educational process in the United States is not.[1]

The Crisis in Professional Education: Another Facet of the Problem

Donald Schon and others have described a crisis in contemporary professional education.[2] Professionals (i.e., those with special training, requisite skills, certification) and the professions to which they belong are accused of (1) self-seeking at the expense of clients and the public at large, (2) the ignoring of social service, which is a societal expectation of the professions, (3) a failure to police themselves effectively, and (4) no real interest in the values they promote. Indeed, professionals such as doctors, lawyers, and the clergy have experienced a drop in prestige by the public.

Also falling under this general blanket of criticism are the professional schools, including seminaries. These schools do not appear to be teaching, or at least are not producing, graduates who can think and act the way professionals are supposed to think and act. New graduates have no ability to deal with crises, with change, with conflict of values, with uncertainty. Put another way, graduates have no ability to relate their fields of expertise to the everyday life of medicine, of architecture, of the Church. It is no wonder, then, in hearing these criticisms from the public they serve and to whom they are responsible, that many professional schools have adopted integration as a byword, a slogan, and a goal.[3]

---

1. It does not seem to matter who is president or what party is in power, the issue of education is always a major one in the rhetoric of campaigns, and thereafter in the White House. The real issue, however, is how much money and attention is finally given to constructive progress toward solving some long-standing problems.

2. See chapters 3 and 7 in this volume.

3. Integration of theory and praxis, of the church and the world, of head and heart, of the vagaries of real-life situations with the knowledge of particular professions—all of this and more is called for. And the focus on spirituality and wholeness, or *paideia* and formation, also calls for integration.

Central to understanding the present crisis in the educating of professionals is recognizing the bifurcation of theory and praxis.[4] Professional schools argue that theory is most important. This is reflected in the status accorded to theory teachers and the place of theoretical disciplines in the curriculum. The other side of the coin is that praxis is undervalued in teaching and in the curriculum. Education in such an environment consists essentially of learning theory and then a few techniques necessary to apply it to particular situations.

The result, according to Schon and others, is fairly clear: Theory and a "few" techniques are highly valued, while the ability to adapt and apply theory is not. But what happens when the graduate of such a professional school is found in a situation that is new, that does not quite fit the theory, that calls for new or adapted techniques? This question is at the heart of the professional's life, for such new circumstances represent about 90 percent of the working day. The professional functions here in situations where a knowledge of the past and some important experience are confronted by the new, the uncertain, the challenging. How do we make professional decisions in such circumstances? How do instructors in professional schools teach this? These questions, so many contemporary critics would argue, are rarely if ever addressed by professional schools.[5] This is not just a problem for professional schools but for society and the communities they serve. The roles of priests, doctors, lawyers, and others as technicians or as experts with all the theory to answer the questions of contemporary life do not seem to work anymore.

Religious Education in the Church: A Variation on a Societal Theme

Virtually all churches proclaim loudly that education is an important part of their mission, of their reason for being, of their future. The Episcopal Church, for example, has labeled it as a "mission imperative," and other denominations use similar rhetoric. In many churches, Sunday school attendance is seen to be more important and meaningful than attendance at the worship service, for adults and children alike. If one has to choose between going to Sunday school or the main worship service, many would choose the former. Education is said to represent a process and a content central to the

---

4. Cf. chapter 7.

5. See Donald Schon, *The Reflective Practitioner* (New York: Basic Books, 1982), 3–20.

church's identity, to what it is called to be and do. It is a fundamental activity of the Church and of other faith communities everywhere. It should, therefore, have special priority when the resources of the Church, both human and financial, are considered.

But when the actual work of the Church is evaluated, a mirror image of our larger society is created. If Americans speak highly of the value of education, the status of schools everywhere speaks another message. So it is also with the Church. It would seem that the Church has not yet responded to its mission imperative. Whether we speak of entering seminarians or of active lay people in the church, there is an acknowledged illiteracy of the Bible, of Church history, of theology and ethics, of liturgy. At the seminary level, virtually all denominations are facing cutbacks or trying to maintain the status quo in the light of dwindling dollars. On a positive note, we could be asking the creative question: How best may we use limited resources? On a negative note, the question may actually be: Which seminary wants or needs to die for the sake of the continuation of others? On the local level, finding teachers to teach seminary classes, Sunday school classes, or adult education classes is a very difficult problem. This is not simply because there may not be competent people but also because there may be a genuine lack of interest. As with education in secular America, and despite all the rhetoric about the value and need for education, the issues of creating motivation and of finding people who actually want to teach is critical for the Church.

There are, of course, many proposed solutions for this education- al dilemma. Assuming that we accept education as a priority, then one simple solution is to provide more money for educational programs. In some instances this has actually occurred (e.g., ethnic programs), but by and large it has not. Perhaps we should bite the bullet and have fewer but better seminaries. Or again, perhaps the answer for the Church lies in new curricula, at once more pertinent, more compre- hensive, and more creative.

The question remains: How are we to make education a priority in a society that, for all of its rhetoric, does not seem to value education? Even if we in the Church had consensus about the general value of education, what content, what methods, and what purposes would we be able to agree upon as we worked toward implementation? In the midst of a diverse and pluralistic society searching for consensus, the Church is doing the same. How are we to achieve this? In moving toward a solution, I do not propose to give the answer but rather to identify some of the variables that must be considered.

The goal must be clearly identified. What do we want? Education is a means to an end, not an end in itself. We learn skills (reading, writing, pastoral listening, etc.), but these are not enough. We acquire all sorts of knowledge of the Bible, of church history, of theology, of a book of worship services and liturgy, but this is not enough. Rather, what Christians hope for is to bring the Christian faith (content and skills, theory and praxis) into dialogue with all facets of our everyday lives. We seek this so that we can live and work faithfully in the world God has given us—to serve our society, yes, but to do it from the perspective of our faith, to be informed by its values and worldview. How will we achieve such a broad and ambitious goal? First, we must take the nature of our world seriously. That is usually not very hard to do. But perhaps what is called for is a communal consciousness that this must occur. Second, we must also take the nature of the Church, at all levels, seriously. Pluralism and diversity characterize the Church. This diversity often causes conflicts over worship, sexuality, budgets, and everything else. But to be pluralistic and diverse is to be a microcosm of the world we live in. In other words, taking the world and the Church seriously and exploring ways in which they are connected and ways in which they influence one another, these must be undertaken and accomplished before the distinctiveness of the Church and its educational mission can be fully articulated. If we choose to value education, we must understand that such a choice may be a countercultural activity. As such, it may not receive affirmation by all members of the Church or wider society.

What results or goals does pursuing educational priorities fulfill? Though not an end in itself, education can be a means to approach questions that confront the Church. Questions of identity: Who are we? Questions of stability: How do we build or maintain a foundation as the people of God? Questions of continuity: Where are we going and how is this related to where we have been? And, most important, questions of mission: What are we to do? These are large and important questions. Lifting up education as a central priority within the Church is critically important if we are to address these questions responsibly. To do so means we must take seriously the particularity of our Christian community as a gathered body with a long history and with scripture in its midst. This helps both to explain the Church's present situation and to define the way it can act in the future. Ecclesiastes says "there is nothing new under the sun" (1:9).

Our problems are not necessarily new or unique. Perhaps we can learn from others who have come before us, even from those who lived in times as far removed from us as the biblical writers.

Scriptural Community: A Perspective from Which to Understand Education in the Church

There is a biblical mandate for education. The following passages illustrate a concern for education found in all three parts of the Hebrew Bible.

Torah
And these words which I command you this day shall be upon your heart; and you shall teach them diligently to your children, and shall talk of them when you sit in your house, and when you walk by the way, and when you lie down, and when you rise. And you shall bind them as a sign upon your hand, and they shall be as frontlets between your eyes. And you shall write them on the doorposts of your house and on your gates. (Deut 6:6–9, RSV)

Prophets
Come, let us go up to the mountain of the LORD,
    to the house of the God of Jacob;
that he may teach us his ways
    and that we may walk in his paths. (Isa 2:3, RSV)

Writings
My child, do not forget my teaching,
    but let your heart keep my commandments;
for length of days and years of life
    and abundant welfare will they give you.

Do not let loyalty and faithfulness forsake you;
    bind them around your neck,
    write them on the tablet of your heart.
So you will find favor and good repute
    in the sight of God and of people. (Prov 3:1–4, NRSV)

The call is clear for education, teaching, and learning; these "mission imperatives" are found in all parts of the biblical witness. But, as with our contemporary society, clarity about the goal, about the priority, is not always enough.

One particular biblical period is especially instructive and illustrative of the problem facing a scriptural community with a mandate for education. The postexilic period of ancient Israel[6] is the first time we can begin to assume a majority of the texts we now call scripture were written and were being used by most of the people. This was a gradual process and was not finally completed until rabbinic (Jewish) and patristic (Christian) times.[7] At the beginning of the postexilic period, many texts were not yet written or were in an uncertain and fluid state, depending on which community we speak of. Within many communities (e.g., Babylon, Egypt, Jerusalem) where Jews now resided there was a religious pluralism so extreme it threatened the very continuity of Israel. There was no single definition of Israel, no single notion of how Israel should be constituted, or should relate to foreign powers, or should govern itself. The identity of Israel was a central question. Was Israel the territories that had recently fallen to Babylon and were now under the control of the Persians, or could an Israelite live in Babylon or Egypt? How did these Diaspora communities relate to Jerusalem and the land of Israel? These questions were at the heart of the exile and its aftermath, and there was no one answer capable of providing consensus.[8] Perhaps most importantly, there was no single definition of God. There were many visions and many messengers, some of whom proclaimed that God wanted Israel to return to old ways of doing things while others had new and revolutionary programs and visions to share.[9]

To a great extent, the religious pluralism of the early postexilic period can be explained by and be related to new societal circumstances. The cult, which had been virtually destroyed, was trying to reestablish itself and its authority. There was no king, no monarchical state. There was no autonomy of the people, and this was clearly not going to change in the foreseeable future. There was the Diaspora, the dispersion of many people to Babylon primarily, but also to Egypt and

---

6. This period is usually dated from the time of the rebuilding of the Temple and the edict of Cyrus allowing exiles to return, to the time of Roman occupation, that is, roughly the last half of the sixth century B.C.E. to the first century B.C.E.

7. See Philip R. Davies, *Scribes and Schools: The Canonization of the Hebrew Scriptures,* Library of Ancient Israel (Louisville, Ky.: Westminster John Knox, 1998), and other works cited therein.

8. Cf. the recent autobiographical study by Edward Said for a powerful account of the effects of "exile" in the contemporary period (*Out of Place* [New York: Random House, 1999]).

9. See the discussion of these messengers in Paul Hanson, *The Dawn of Apocalyptic: The Historical and Social Roots of Jewish Apocalyptic Eschatology* (Philadelphia: Fortress, 1979).

elsewhere. Never again would all the worshipers of Yahweh live in the same land. Never again would the nation of Israel have direct control over all Jews. In this period, many different leaders and visionaries had many hopes for the future as well as nostalgia about the past. The society of ancient Israel was changing, searching for consensus and identity in radically new circumstances. Religious institutions and leaders were influenced by all of this, at once symptomatic of the changes occurring and also helping to shape the people's response.

Despite differences in theological, social, and political points of view, despite the arguments about identity and the different physical locations for Israel, the postexilic communities did share something in common. This commonness, the matrix for the pluralism of this period, was a dialogue between text (scripture) and community. In this period, scriptural community was born. One facet of that pluralism was the existence of serious questions concerning identity, continuity with the past, stability, and mission. There was no geographical, theological, or experiential unity. But these communities did share two things. First, they shared a text that was perceived to be authoritative in some way, a text consisting of Torah, then later the Prophets, and finally, much later still, the Writings. Second, these postexilic communities shared a mandate regarding the text and reflected by the illustrative passages cited above—a mandate to remember, to teach, to preserve, to relate the text to their circumstances, and to live by.

To identify the matrix of emergent scriptural communities in the postexilic period is not to remove all problems. The text had different versions in different communities. The text meant, as it does today, everything to everyone. Nevertheless, no one could ignore it. Thus, postexilic Israel, whether in Jerusalem, Babylon, or Egypt, shared an interaction between the text and the problems of the day. This shared interaction was and is the glue of scriptural community.

Not surprisingly, the pluralism of the postexilic world and of the scriptures produced many different visions, many different ways to be God's people. Finally, those ways became our contemporary ways. In light of our present needs, we will focus on one group, one way found in the postexilic period: the way of the wise, the sages. Their agenda, education, teaching, and concern are also ours. We must remember, however, that this is only one of many ways in which education and the mission of the people may be viewed. We are heirs to other ways that must, finally, be integrated into an overall view of biblical education and its pertinence for today.

Wisdom and Education in the Church: An Overview

What do the wisdom writers and teachers care about? What is most valuable to them as they address educational concerns in ancient Israel? Though these sages do not address this latter question in the way contemporary educational summits do, the wisdom writings make their priorities clear.

The purpose of education and learning for biblical sages is to live well in the world God has given to us. This will not necessarily mean wealth or health, but it will mean living in accord with the intentions of God as they are manifested in the structures of the created world. No wonder that by the end of the postexilic period these sages will become interpreters of the Torah, a primary source of God's revealed will.[10]

The starting point for education and learning, for living well, is experience. Simply put, we learn how to live well by living. Therefore, everyday life is where we begin and where we end. How can we decide which roads lead to disaster and which lead to success? Experience is a vital component in making those judgments and decisions. Beginning then, with our own experience and that of others (crystallized in the form of proverbs, in the counsel of friends, in the mandates of the good and wise king), the task of education is to use our reason as we address questions about good and right living. We are to observe the world carefully, searching for causes and effects, formulating theories of action to test them, and finally reflecting on our practice, on our living. For example, how does a priest deal with a crisis? How does anyone? What values are reflected? What changes, or does not, in our response as Christians, as members of a community of faith, when any particular issue is addressed? This kind of questioning and self-conscious, even introspective, reflection on the world we live in and on our behavior patterns and values always takes seriously the social matrix in which we find ourselves. This process is at the heart of the educational process of the sage.[11]

The biblical sage, like us, does not begin with a clean slate, with no presuppositions or values. We have seen one basic presupposition, that there is an order in the world. However dimly it manifests itself, our job is to discern that order and to teach each other how to live in accord

---

10. See chapter 1.

11. See James Crenshaw, *Education in Ancient Israel: Across the Deadening Silence* (New York: Doubleday, 1998); and Gerhard von Rad, *Wisdom in Ancient Israel* (Nashville: Abingdon, 1972).

with it. A second presupposition, concerning authority, has hierarchical social implications: There are those who know more about the order of the world than others. Learn from them. Searching for wisdom, for the rhyme and reason of the order of the world, will enable us to live well. This search is a moral issue for the sages. It is not optional.

Thus far, the educational concerns and methods of the biblical sages could be an apologia for many types of secular education. But the rationale of education for the sage rests on theological foundations, even if they are often not explicitly cited in the aphoristic literature produced by them. The order of the world is a created order. It is the order of the creator, God, that we seek to find and that we presuppose lies behind and within, permeating in every way the world we live in. The authority of the sage, based on knowledge and experience, is given by God. Reason is also a gift. It is in using reason that we fulfill God's intention, learn to make sense of our experience, and live well. In the process of discerning order, we clearly must discern between good and evil (Gen 3). That ability to discern is both an ability and a responsibility, given by God. We will be held accountable by God and the world for how well we exercise that ability. No wonder the sages are moralistic about this. For them, it is an either/or very much like the either/or of Deuteronomy or Elijah; life and death are at stake in the decision made. And God wishes life.

The sages are involved in a nonoptional search for wisdom and in teaching it to Israel for the purposes of faithful living. This search is in response to a biblical mandate that continues to this day. The search is not always easy. The order in the world is not often clearly perceived or always clearly visible. God is not always easily understood or perceived in light of the nature of the world we live in. But the search is mandated, and the text is a repository of the past and a container of directions for the future. The text is an indicator of clues to God and order. It is a common starting point.

The writings of the sages in the Bible are mainly concerned with issues of everyday life versus the problems of the cult or religious establishment. This observation is critically important, for there are serious implications here for the way we in the twenty-first century should approach educational concerns. First, it is in everyday experience that we must see God and order: in computers, in streets filled with the homeless, in football, in war, in strife, in political contests. Second, a call to find and embrace wisdom requires that we take the world and the wisdom found within it seriously. Finally, education in the Church, so these sages would tell us, is not just learning the story of our past or even distilling its values for our lives. It is reflecting on our world in a conscious, intentional way, bringing every bit of what we already know of who God is and how God acts into dialogue with that world in order to live faithfully into the future. Yes, we must know the story and the stipulations (Torah), but they become quickly sterile and irrelevant without the world we live in as a part of the mix of education.

Toward the Future

In light of these observations about education in our society, in the Church, and in the world of the biblical sages, where are we to go and what are we to do? The task would seem to identity and name the problem of education, to determine what it actually is before we attempt to solve it.

To be involved in the interaction between scripture and community is one way to begin to identify and name the problem. Whatever else happens, we need to be in dialogue with scriptural values if the particularity of a Christian mandate for education is to be meaningful. The sages of ancient Israel in the postexilic period were involved in the same type of dialogue, with the same issues at stake: identity, continuity, and mission. The value for understanding our present situation in light of this analogy with the sages of ancient Israel affirms the "there is nothing new under the sun" of Ecclesiastes and at the same time challenges us to learn more.

The sages and their literature represent one of many responses to the question, What difference does it make that we are a scriptural community? They provide a valuable perspective as we seek to understand and carry out our contemporary educational task. With the problem understood, we have further questions. First, the issue of resources: What was the role of the sage in education? How does that role help us today? Second, a question of method: How did the sage teach? Can the methods used by biblical sages help us in our very different world?[12]

Regardless of the answers to these questions, the sages make the world our educational context. They refuse to let us separate our faith from it. They urge us to search for God in everyday life, knowing at times we will be left with frustration and agony at the mystery of God's ways. They celebrate life given and the tasks to which we are all called, especially education.

---

12. See, e.g., chapter 11, pp. 140–43.

CHAPTER 10

The Sages and Contemporary Education in the Church

W e live in a world that cries out for education. In the Church, as a scriptural community, one answer to this cry is to be found in a dialogue between the text, with its particular stories, values, and stipulations, and the community, with its special problems, new revelations, and challenges. One special resource in addressing the issue of education in the Church and in our society is the body of wisdom writers and teachers of ancient Israel. The points of view and the educational agenda of these teachers and writers must be brought into dialogue with the twenty-first century.

My present goals are modest. By attempting to identify the roles and locations of the ancient and contemporary sage, I seek to understand how they can help us deal with the mandate and concomitant problems of education. How do they go about the task of teaching? How might we?

Wisdom in the World: What Are We Looking For?

Sages are perceived to have wisdom and/or are engaged in a search for it. Before we can look for the sages, we need to know a little about the object they seek and the process they are engaged in. This will allow us to recognize sages when we see them.

My son, if you receive my words and treasure up my command-
ments with you,
making your ear attentive to wisdom
and inclining your heart to understanding;
yes, if you cry out for insight
and raise your voice for understanding,
if you seek it like silver
and search for it as for hidden treasures;
then you will understand the fear of the LORD
and find the knowledge of God.
For the LORD gives wisdom;
from his mouth come knowledge and understanding;
he stores up sound wisdom for the upright;
he is a shield to those who walk in integrity,
guarding the paths of justice
and preserving the way of his saints.
Then you will understand righteousness and justice
and equity, every good path;
for wisdom will come into your heart,
and knowledge will be pleasant to your soul;
discretion will watch over you,
understanding will guard you;
delivering you from the way of evil,
from men of perverted speech,
who forsake the paths of uprightness
to walk in the ways of darkness,
who rejoice in doing evil,
and delight in the perverseness of evil;
men whose paths are crooked,
and who are devious in their ways. (Prov 2:1–15, RSV)

This passage both describes and mandates the search for wisdom and is given by either a father or king to his son or subjects.
The search must begin with recognition of the sources. First, the
teacher who mandates the search stands in authority over the
student/child/subject. Second, God is the ultimate source and
giver of wisdom. The motivation is both intellectual and emo-
tional. If it achieves good results, the search will provide the
searcher with protection from evil, will affirm the searcher is on
the right (good) path rather than the wrong (evil) path, allowing

the searcher to live well. For this sage, searching for wisdom is a worthwhile pursuit and goal for life, and achieving that goal is very possible indeed.

> When I applied my mind to know wisdom, and to see the business that is done on earth, how one's eyes see sleep neither day nor night, then I saw all the work of God, that no one can find out what is happening under the sun. However much they may toil in seeking, they will not find it out; even though those who are wise claim to know, they cannot find it out. (Eccl 8:16–17, NRSV)

Here again a biblical sage, Ecclesiastes, describes a search for wisdom. But this search appears to be doomed to failure. The author does not deny there are wise people in the world, perhaps he would even use the term sage, but the search for wisdom is a relative one. Wisdom, if we mean by this complete knowledge and understanding of the ways of the world and of God, is simply not attainable.

> [Job said,] "Surely there is a mine for silver,
>   and a place for gold which they refine.
> Iron is taken out of the earth,
>   and copper is smelted from the ore.
> Men put an end to darkness,
>   and search out to the farthest bound
>   the ore in gloom and deep darkness.
> They open shafts in a valley away from where men live;
>   they are forgotten by travelers,
>   they hang afar from men, they swing to and fro.
> As for the earth, out of it comes bread;
>   but underneath it is turned up as by fire.
> Its stones are the place of sapphires,
>   and it has dust of gold.
>
> "That path no bird of prey knows,
>   and the falcon's eye has not seen it.
> The proud beasts have not trodden it;
>   the lion has not passed over it.
>
> "Man puts his hand to the flinty rock,
>   and overturns mountains by the roots.

He cuts out channels in the rocks,
    and his eye sees every precious thing.
He binds up the streams so that they do not trickle,
    and the thing that is hid he brings forth to light.

"But where shall wisdom be found?
    And where is the place of understanding?
Man does not know the way to it,
    and it is not found in the land of the living.
The deep says, 'It is not in me,'
    and the sea says, 'It is not with me.'
It cannot be gotten for gold,
    and silver cannot be weighed as its price.
It cannot be valued in the gold of Ophir,
    in precious onyx or sapphire.
Gold and glass cannot equal it,
    nor can it be exchanged for jewels of fine gold.
No mention shall be made of coral or of crystal;
    the price of wisdom is above pearls.
The topaz of Ethiopia cannot compare with it,
    nor can it be valued in pure gold.

"Whence then comes wisdom?
    And where is the place of understanding?
It is hid from the eyes of all living,
    and concealed from the birds of the air.
Abaddon and Death say,
    'We have heard a rumor of it with our ears.'

"God understands the way to it,
    and he knows its place.
For he looks to the ends of the earth,
    and sees everything under the heavens.
When he gave to the wind its weight,
    and meted out the waters by measure;
when he made a decree for the rain,
    and a way for the lightning of the thunder;
then he saw it and declared it;
    he established it, and searched it out.
And he said to man,
    'Behold, the fear of the Lord, that is wisdom;
and to depart from evil is understanding.'" (Job 28)

This text represents a combination of the viewpoints expressed in Proverbs and Ecclesiastes. The author acknowledges the source of wisdom, as well as an inability to understand wisdom fully and the need for the search to continue nevertheless. The final result in the book of Job is a confrontation with the source and giver of wisdom itself.

For the biblical writers, wisdom, finally attainable or unattainable, involves a search process that affects both head and heart and demands all the motivation we can muster. Wisdom, however much or little of it we gain, helps us to understand both God and the world, and allows or enables us to live better. Wisdom, from a human perspective, is relative at best. We cannot find or possess it totally. What little we know or do not know comes from experience. Who are those that search for it?

Wisdom in the Contemporary World

One way to address the question of wisdom and sages in contemporary society is to focus on the product and the process of some common activities often associated with special knowledge and expertise.

Product (=Wisdom)	*Process* (=Sage)
Science	Scientists
Skills/techniques	Technicians of every stripe
Critical thinking (=Result)	Academicians, researchers
Spirituality (=integrated life)	Spiritual directors

Although each of these dichotomies differs in character, there are some general observations we may make. Wisdom today as in the past is more than a body of knowledge. To be wise is to be involved in a process of inquiry, to be open to the new[1] and to have knowledge of the old as an invaluable guideline. In this sense, wisdom and the process of seeking it is a mirror image of the community-text dialogue found in scriptural communities of faith.[2] Wisdom, as in biblical times, is skill in living.[3] Finally, wisdom today is competent practice, the ability to do things well, in accord with certain rules, and with good results.

---

1. "The two most important things for our country, and for the world, are the way in which we educate young people and the creation of new ideas," said Lawrence Summers, recently chosen as the president of Harvard University (*New York Times*, 12 March 2001, A8).

2. In this case, however, the searcher and interpreter is the individual, though ideally this person would add to the wisdom of the community.

3. See, e.g., R. B. Y. Scott, *The Way of Wisdom* (New York: Macmillan, 1971), 6ff.

The sages and the wise of today are first people with knowledge. But this is hardly enough. They are people who are askers of questions, who live skillfully, who are integrated head and heart. They are people who are competent in practice. That is, they are people who can relate theory to the questions raised in and by situations of conflict of values and of uniqueness. They are people who are involved in all facets of the world's life and activities—knowledge and wisdom and understanding are, and were, inclusive of this.

The Sages, Then and Now

Sages in Biblical Times

When sages are identified in the Old Testament they are usually associated with one of four different types of individuals. First, sages are often seen as elders, as heads of families, as the ones most experienced with life and therefore potentially most able to provide instruction and to convey the knowledge necessary for skillful living.

Second, sages are sometimes associated with the monarchy, either the king himself (e.g., Solomon, the paragon and paradigm of all wisdom seekers and finders) or his advisors, those versed in the knowledge of politics, social issues, foreign affairs, and of worldly things. Such counselors were vital for the running of the state.

Third, we may speak generally of sages as teachers and poets. We mean by this designation those who write and use the aphoristic literature. It has been suggested that the students of the teachers of proverbs were royal counselors and others involved in governmental service. It is also frequently suggested that these counselors were also the authors and teachers. By the second century B.C.E. and the time of Ben Sira, there was clearly a group of teachers, sages, who were to be distinguished from royal counselors of times past. It is probably such a group of writers and teachers who were responsible for the composition of Proverbs, Job, and Ecclesiastes.

Fourth, scribes (Hebrew, *sopherim*) are often counted among the sages. These are the record keepers, the writers of contracts, of treaties, of stories (e.g., perhaps the Joseph story [Gen 37–50] or the succession narrative [2 Sam 9–20; 1 Kgs 1–2]). In the postexilic period as emergent scripture became centrally important, the scribes were charged with its transmission and often its interpretation.

Many different functions and roles are associated with the figure of the sage. Although by the postexilic period the primary sages were either the poet-teachers of proverbial literature or the scribes in charge of textual transmission and sometimes interpretation, the family and royal roots of the sage cannot be forgotten.[4] Indeed, the authority structures and the social structures of the postexilic period were very much dependent upon family and monarchy models. The activities associated with the sage varied considerably: general advice, moral injunction, intellectual questioning, teaching, political involvement, composition, preservation, interpretation, and intimate knowledge of sacred and secular texts. The activities of the sage occurred in all parts of ancient Israel's world, not merely or even primarily in the cult.

Sages in Our Times

If we ask the question, "Who are the sages today?" what might be the response? Would people identify as modern sages the clergy, those who are teachers, preachers, and who are experienced with God and the Church? Bishops and others higher up in the hierarchies of the Church may then warrant special attention because their respective denominational bodies have recognized them as having special knowledge, experience, skills, or a relationship with God, the giver of wisdom.

Perhaps we might hear the suggestion that professional theologians, writers, and teachers are the sages. The deep thinkers, the experts in book knowledge and teaching skills, also might be considered contemporary sages. Or again, the answer might include prominent and active lay people, those who have been successful in the world of politics and business. Such people are often considered to have special authority and knowledge. They are often asked to address gatherings and to lead task forces and other groups.

Notice that all of the sages identified to this point are not only members of our particular faith community, but are usually prominent and active members. Occasionally, if we are Christians, we might consider other Christians outside our community and, once in a great while, even a non-Christian whose work is seen as pertinent to issues facing the Church and society. However, when the lists of speakers and teachers for conferences held by churches are examined, we find very few sages from this latter category represented.

If, however, we took our cue from biblical sages, what might the sages of today look like? It is doubtful the clergy would be highly visible, for they were not in biblical times. Professional theologians and

---

4. See James Crenshaw, *Education in Ancient Israel: Across the Deadening Silence* (New York: Doubleday, 1998).

successful lay people probably would not be consulted, primarily because we have difficulty finding biblical analogues at all. On the other hand, sages who have expertise in all parts of the society (e.g., politics, medicine, law) but who have little or nothing to do with the organization of the cult are the ones with the clearest analogues in biblical times.

Clearly, contemporary and biblical societies are very different. It is a fair assumption that most sages in ancient Israel knew of and were affected by the cult. Today, members of analogous groups (successful politicians, doctors, lawyers, scientists) are often not even members of the Church and certainly not very knowledgeable about it. If we limit our definition of sages to those who know the Church, its structures, and its values intimately, then the scope of our resources is dramatically lessened. We have also made a break with the biblical tradition.

If, finally, we in the Church affirm the need, with ancient Israel, to have sages from all parts of the world and its life, then somehow we will need to find a way to relate the knowledge and skill in living that they possess to our text and traditions in the Church. We will need to broaden our notion of education in the Church to include areas that are now tangential, irrelevant, or simply mystifying to those sages within it. This can be threatening and scary, for the inquiries that sages outside the Church today engage in and the knowledge they possess raise serious, not easily answered questions about God and about our community.[5] On the other hand, not to broaden our notion of sages is also dangerous, for this excludes God and our Church world from the world of politics, science, and much of what is going on in the created order. This is something the sages of ancient Israel would tell us we cannot, must not, do.

The Sages, Then and Now: Revisited

Sages in Biblical Times

It is not difficult to determine the location of the activities of biblical sages: the family or clan, the palace, the court, and finally, by the time of Ben Sira, the school. The wisdom literature itself, especially Proverbs and the collection process that must be presupposed for

---

5. Some of these potential sages for the Church are former, now disaffected, members of the community. They have their own questions to bring to the Church, to relate to the scriptural and other traditions of the past. Sometimes the lack of receptiveness on the part of the Church has driven such sages away. To now value these same folks is to be open to the new and, in some cases, even to a reversal of previous behavior and attitude.

this book, would seem to argue for the existence of some institution with pedagogical intentions. Since the time for the final collection of Proverbs is almost always set within the postexilic period, we will assume schools and sages within them from this period, in all probability before Jesus ben Sira.

In the postexilic period we may also come to speak of sages in the cultic establishment. With the cultic hierarchy under Ezra, it is understandable that the cult would contain those who were considered wise by most within the society. With cultic officials rather than the monarch as the center of the social organization, this is a logical and almost inevitable development. Evidence for the placement of sages within the cult comes from wisdom psalms, usually attributed to the postexilic period. In addition, the Torah psalms (especially Ps 119) display formal characteristics (e.g., acrostic structures) that are characteristic of particularly literate composers such as devoted and learned scribes. Finally, the equation of Torah with Wisdom in Ecclesiasticus (e.g., 24:23) surely points to a merging of the locus of wisdom and cult.

Sages in Our Times

Where do we in the Church find our sages today? As we noted above, we will certainly find some of them in the institutional Church itself. We often speak primarily of professionals and mean by this term those who are employed by the institution and have some special skills associated with its effective running. In some instances we will identify those who have a special relationship to (e.g., leadership) and commitment to (e.g., vows of obedience) the institution, namely, the clergy. The family, such an important place to find the wise in ancient Israel, is not as readily and automatically associated with the sage in contemporary American society. This represents an important shift in cultural and societal norms and values. If we search for other places where the Church recognizes sages, we will be drawn to educational institutions (universities, seminaries, schools of other varieties, study centers [most often run by the Church itself], and the business world). Most often, those perceived as sages by the Church will be members of the Church itself. Moreover, these sages usually reflect the biblical wisdom that success (i.e., money, status, leadership) represents a life lived well. It is these people, with money, status, and leadership responsibilities, who function as sages today, drawn primarily from the membership of the Church. They are often on center stage when education is discussed in and for the Church.

Of course, we need knowledge of the world and knowledge of the text and the Church's traditions—so the sages of ancient Israel would tell us. But where are we to find them when the world of the Church and the world of society are not the same? How are we to relate them?

Sages and the Educational Process Today: Implications

We today are like the sages of ancient Israel: searching for wisdom and addressing important questions concerning teaching and learning. What do we really need? Where shall we find wisdom? When we look at the radically different nature of the contemporary world versus the biblical world, how are we to appropriate and make sense of the biblical mandate for education? With the breakdown of the nuclear family unit, where will wisdom be found? With the Church as disestablished, as separated from the wisdom of the world and its sages, what is to be done? How can or how should this wisdom of the world, these sages, become a part of our educational processes and even our goals?

Bringing the World to the Church: A Mandate of the Wise of Ancient Israel

If we are to emulate and follow the sages of Israel, we must locate and use the wise of society (from politics, from science, from technology) and listen to their educational agenda. These contemporary sages will often ask questions or raise issues we do not wish to hear; but listening to them and making their experience of the world and its order part of our experience is a mandate from Israelite sages. In doing this, we must be aware that sages are sometimes advocates of change and intervention, calling for transformation of existing paradigms and raising important, and often disturbing, questions. To be in the company of such sages is not always comfortable, but it is a nonoptional part of the mandate of biblical wisdom.

In receiving the knowledge of contemporary sages, and especially from those parts of the created order of which the Church has little knowledge and experience, we must build a new foundation, or strengthen an existing one, that is capable of hearing the dreams of a new future. Such dreams may come from radical proponents of feminism, or from scientists with new definitions of and experiences with life (in test tubes, in gene research), or from other sages in our world. We must be open and ready to hear such new visions and to put them into dialogue with the traditions of the community of faith in the Church.

Toward New Roles for Sages in the Church

If we respond to the mandate contained within the teachings and examples of the biblical sages, what will the sages in the Church look like? How will they change? How might they stay the same? We begin with the presupposition that the Church does have sages. Most of these sages are more knowledgeable of the text part of the text-community dynamic, that is, they know the biblical traditions, the history of the Church, and the other parts of the Church's life. At the same time, these sages of the Church and of its text can and must help relate the sages of the world to the community of the text, for this is an all-important part of education for a scriptural community. If the community lacks a deep knowledge of the world, new roles may be necessary for the sage within the Church. Rather than speaking definitively of the Church, which represents a rather small world, the sage within the Church may need to think of new roles, new functions, and new paradigms for living out whatever it means to be wise in contemporary society. Through all of this, reflection on experience, skillful living, competent practice, and the relating of the values of text and tradition to the changing circumstances of the world remain constant and enduring characteristics of the sage, biblical and contemporary.

One of the new roles for the Church sage may require him or her to be the nonexpert. This is not a passive responsibility or merely a confession of ignorance; rather, it calls for the ability to relate two different but essential facets of the educational process. First, taking seriously the community and the world, the Church sage must call for recognition that much knowledge of that world is not possessed by the Church itself. The sage must argue instead that wisdom will be found with other sages far more knowledgeable of the world. At the same time, such knowledge must be related to the textual traditions of the scriptural community with their affirmation of the truth that wisdom finally comes from God and is always, to some extent, shrouded in mystery.

Another new role for the sage in the Church might be teaching through mimicry or illustration. Here the goal is to teach people how to be skillful in living through living itself rather than through application of the most current theory (scientific or theological or otherwise) to particular situations. To be successful with such a role, the sage must recognize there is no one way to do things, no one answer.

Finally, sages may be reflectors on practice.[6] The goal is to encourage and even teach self-conscious reflective inquiry on behavior. The

---

6. See, e.g., chapter 3 above.

sage must identify and be sensitive to the variables within the specific community (e.g., text, liturgy) and the variables outside the community as well (e.g., societal goals and issues). Both sets of variables must be taken seriously if wise action is to be achieved and if reflection on practice is to occur effectively. What is called for is a balancer, an ascertainer of what is at issue, a perceptive and sensitive listener, a facilitator of communication between different parties, different values, different variables. This is a challenging picture of the Church's sage and the educational mission for the Church of the twenty-first century.

Church Sages and Inquiry: Toward a Partial Relativity

The wisdom of biblical sages calls us to be open to the world of non-Church experts in a wide variety of disciplines and areas, and calls us to be open to new arguments, new values, and new worldviews. We are forced to recognize that we can too easily become prisoners of our little worlds, with the Church defining their boundaries. Such smallness and narrowness is detrimental to education biblically conceived.

Within the Church, the sage must search for the common matrix upon which its pluralism exists, while recognizing diversity and building it firmly into the educational process. This may lead to some relativism, that is, some recognition that there is more than one way to live out the Christian mandate within human community. All of this is finally reflected in the Bible itself with its many different conceptions of community and of education.[7] These differences represent the results of many dialogues between communities and texts in biblical times, which we, as communities of the word, continue to reflect in the present day.

Church Sages: Constancy and Stability

If part of the function of the sage is to recognize and even embrace a certain type of relativism, it is also the contemporary sage's responsibility to provide a stable context for inquiry. In doing this, the sage is to be faithful to unchanging values found in the community-text interchange and dialogue. The sage is called to anchor the moral values in the particular religious community in which she or he lives and works. All is not relative, and this must become an important part of the educational process.

---

7. See, e.g., Walter Brueggemann, *The Creative Word* (Philadelphia: Fortress, 1982).

We are left with an important set of issues. How does the church sage take the knowledge and wisdom of the world seriously, take the world's sages seriously, engage in serious inquiry and reflection with the help of those sages, and still remain true to the community of faith and to the source of wisdom? No matter what solutions or ways of living faithfully are proposed, the final allegiance of the community must be to the source of wisdom—not to the community, not to the text, but to the one who gives community, gives text, and is capable of taking both away.

CHAPTER 11

New Paradigms and Methods
Teaching the Wisdom of Israel in a New Land

W e have discussed the problem of education in the Church and in our society. We have tried to delineate the factors that create the problem and some of the issues and resources that will need to be used in addressing its eventual solution. We have looked at contemporary and biblical mandates for education. Both our secular society and our Christian communities of faith are concerned about education, about effective teaching and learning. The Church is particularly interested in giving each of its members the ability to interrelate ancient stories and stipulations to contemporary concerns, problems, and challenges.

Central to the description of the problem of education for American society and Church in the twenty-first century is recognition of the need for education and not simply the rhetoric calling for it to be good or better or more effective in comparison with other societies. The need for education is grounded not in the desire to be technologically advanced, or to be democratically superior, or to be smartest or richest. Rather, the overall goal of education is to provide the learning and training necessary for citizens and believers to live faithfully and to live well (skillfully) in the world given to us. Education then becomes centrally important to every society and to every community. Education then becomes a central part of the mission of the society and the Church.

We have seen that the problem and character of education is representative and illustrative of the basic nature of a scriptural community. We have a concern to relate our past, concretized in the scriptural text and in other texts and practices, to the present, to the contemporary community of faith and its society. The nature of this scriptural community is very much at the center of a constitutional society or any other body that has authoritative texts and traditions that must necessarily be related to new phenomena and issues within societies. Within the scriptural traditions, this book has focused on the biblical sages and the wisdom literature they produced, with their explicit pedagogical agenda. I have tried to relate that educational agenda to ours, to determine commonness and difference, to see where we might learn from the sages and where we may need to adjust and adapt.

We have addressed the question of resources, particularly those represented by the biblical sages and their contemporary counterparts. These sages, experts in both the texts and traditions of the Church and experts in all facets of knowledge in our world, were easily identified. However, the differences between biblical and contemporary societies created some revealing disparities in the roles and locations of sages. Potential challenges for the present-day Church have been raised. For example, the sages of the Church today are not usually recognized as sages within society at large. This may be due to the place of the Church and religion in the contemporary world. More importantly, for the purposes of education, there appears to be a dividing line, a bifurcation, between the knowledge of the world and the knowledge of the Church. Such a bifurcation did not exist for biblical sages. One way to respond to the biblical mandate for education is to suggest that it should not exist today either. But if we are to use all the sages of the world in our quest to live faithfully and to understand what God is doing, then our communities of faith must be open to hearing their wisdom. This may call for reconceiving the roles of our sages within the Church, seeing them not in terms of expertise and knowledge possessed but rather in terms of openness to the new and ability to coach and to facilitate but not necessarily to have the answer. Such a role as nonexpert for the sage or teacher or professional does not come from the biblical part of the community but from thinkers and critics of education within contemporary society.[1]

---

1. See, e.g., Donald Schon, *The Reflective Practitioner* (New York: Basic Books, 1982); and Jackson Carroll, *Ministry as Reflective Practice: A New Look at the Professional Model* (Washington, D.C.: Alban Institute, 1986).

Our present concern is to ask how the sages taught. To do this we must examine biblical wisdom texts and also the Torah, seeing what was done and why. We must relate these pedagogical concerns and methods to the present day. How do we accomplish our task, being faithful to the mandate from the Bible, which is at the heart of our particularity, our uniqueness, and our mission? At the same time, how do we remain faithful and receptive to the new challenges and gifts God has given us in this time and place that is so different from the biblical communities of old?

How Did the Sages Teach?

The community-text dialogue is usually motivated by a concern to deal with the new, to address problems and challenges not necessarily envisioned or experienced by the biblical authors. This dialogue, this confrontation between old and new, is a central part of the educational task. When the wisdom literature of the sages is evaluated with this in mind, there are several possible models that we may use to conceptualize the pedagogical task and role of the biblical, and contemporary, sage.[2]

1. *The sage-teacher as designer.*[3] Order is critical to the biblical sage; it allows the ability to deal effectively with questions of uncertainty and with conflicts of value. The friends of Job represent a very good example of this. Their notion of order, given by God, allows them to deal with the problems of Job in a fairly straightforward way. An understanding of the way the world has been created and structured is capable of providing explanations and solutions for problems dealing with uncertainty and conflict of values. It is the role of the sage-teacher, as designer, to explicate creation and help us understand its order and rationale. The order of creation is theological in its nature. All our attempts to locate and construct order in our worlds (church, state, family) must take this larger order, given by God, seriously. Therefore, all our attempts to understand creation, to describe and design ways in which the world operates, are finally relativized, for God is the ultimate designer and creator. Thus, whether we look at Job, or Ecclesiastes, or Proverbs, creation and its order are finally veiled in mystery, indeed, a very explicitly theological mystery.

---

2. Some of the following repeats points identified in chapter 3, but the concern here is to generalize and focus on issues of implementation for the Church, versus making pedagogical comparisons between Schon and others and Proverbs.

3. See chapter 3.

Ironically, though the friends of Job try to help him understand, their rigid application of theological order to Job's situation is finally not satisfactory. It is the ability of God to act in different, new, and finally mysterious ways that the friends are unable, or unwilling, to accept.

2. *The sage as user of repertoires of images, maxims, values.* We speak not of sage as author, then, but of teachers who are aware and knowledgeable of a wide number of metaphors and other descriptive images and maxims. The sage does not create the images and traditions, but combines them in new ways in order to sensitize students, to aid and facilitate understanding. These sage-teachers call for all of us to do likewise. From our own expertise and experience we are challenged to discern order, utilizing whatever repertoires of images, values, and metaphors we have as we teach and learn from one another.

3. *The sage-teacher as a setter of the problem.*[4] The sage-teacher is not necessarily a giver of answers but rather someone who frames a problem by providing a picture of the world within which the problem can and should be addressed. We have seen many ways by which the sage does this framing: sometimes with explicitly theological statements and values, sometimes through the retributional (two-ways) system of rewards and punishment, and so on. The sage uses many different forms, both literary and oral, to accomplish this task. The wisdom produced is at once affirmative of many foundational institutions in the culture as one source of support and definition. The wisdom also posits that a larger, less predictable, but finally more reliable source is at the center of our ability to define and act upon particular challenges of life. In light of this wisdom, which hopefully provides an adequate means by which to understand behavior, the student (hearer) will know what resources to draw on in light of the circumstances confronting her. Sometimes this might be a priest, or a family elder, or a king, or a spouse.

4. *The sage as part of the community of inquiry.* The literature of the biblical sages reflects a common theological base and common values for beginning to understand what it means to be wise and foolish in society. In addition, all wisdom literature reflects a commitment to debate, to question, to think within such a context. This commitment comes primarily from the experience of the world. But the theological presuppositions behind the created order, which many biblical sages seek to describe, testify to the sages being a part of the community of faith. The final proof of such an assertion would appear to

---

4. See chapter 3.

be the inclusion of this literature in the Bible as a part of the community's book of faith.

5. *Teachers as creators and participants in a virtual world.*[5] The educational world of the sage and student helps us to address the problems and dilemmas we face. The activity of the teacher-sage is not theoretical and detached, for all of this is done to enable us to deal with the new that confronts us but that must be seen in light of the old if we are to continue to be a scriptural community. The old, the tradition, provides some of the generative metaphors that draw and structure the world, within which we must deal with the new of today.

The Problem of Education: Sage-Teachers and Torah

Postexilic sages are knowledgeable of and informed by Torah and other forms of authoritative scripture available to the particular communities of faith where they live. These sages are also informed by and aware of the world, the problems it creates, and the challenges it provides for the community of faith with a scriptural text. The sages are informed by the mandate for education found in a wide variety of authoritative texts, including wisdom literature, and are aware of the call to relate Torah to the world. I have presupposed that the sages may also be informed by the structure of scripture itself, with its heavy priority on Torah and then the Prophets, and the particular relationship of old/text and new/prophetic message contained within that structure.[6]

The interpretive and educational process found within the structure of Torah itself serves as a paradigm for all future generations, providing the rationale for sages and all within the community of faith.[7] This is what the community of inquiry between teacher and student is about. The sage provides structures of authority and order that are compatible, if not congruent in terms of language and setting, with those of Torah. The sage-teachers are engaged in the same reflective process as found in the Torah: translating and reflecting continually on a textual knowing-in-action or practice in the light of new situations that challenge its values and applicability, and question the uniqueness and the importance of the particularity of the old. All of this is done as part of ancient Israel's response to the mandate to teach and to learn. In doing this, whether as a priest in the

---

5. See chapter 3.

6. For one example of this type of canonical analysis, see my *Between Text and Community: The "Writings" in Canonical Scripture* (Minneapolis: Fortress, 1990).

7. See chapter 3.

Torah or a sage with biblical aphoristic poetry in Proverbs, the text continues to live in the community.

Education, both teaching and learning, as seen from this perspective is not merely or primarily concerned with memorizing stories or laws as an end in itself. Rather, it is a process by which the text is allowed to speak to the present day, a method of searching for ways of living faithfully with the God who gives order and brings life. This is what sages and all the community of faith do in searching for wisdom. Little wonder, then, that the sages become expositors of the Torah, that all Torah, both written and oral, is seen to come from Moses and is tied to a reflective process that is so much a part of the educational agenda of the biblical sages.

The Church and the Wisdom of the Sages

What We Share

With the sages of biblical Israel, we continue to be a part of a community of inquiry. We are challenged, even mandated, to bring the new to the process (e.g., technological change, different values), that is, the insights and concerns of the world we live in. We must also bring the text to the process. Though our views of it can and will change, the text provides stability, a common point of reference for all the diversity of interpretation we teach.

We also share with the sages and teachers of the Bible the mandate to teach and to learn. Scripture has this process and mandate built into its very canonical structure. This is true not only for Torah[8] but for the entire Bible, as the following schematic reflects.[9]

Old	New	
Genesis–Numbers	+ Deuteronomy	= Torah
Torah	+ Prophets	= postexilic canon
Torah and Prophets	+ Writings	= Tanak/Hebrew Bible
Tanak	+ New Testament	= Christian Bible
Bible and tradition	+ new challenges today	= new formulations about social issues, sexuality, etc.

---

8. See the application of a contemporary educational paradigm to the structure of Torah in chapter 3.

9. This schematic can include all kinds of written traditions that become normative and then usually function as lenses through which to understand earlier tradition. So, for example, the Old Testament is read through the perspective of the New Testament for Christians, the Hebrew Bible is read through the perspective of the normative rabbinic tradition for Jews, and so on. See my *Between Text and Community*, 117ff., for further examples.

We also share with ancient sages the problems inherent in the system of interpretation, of relating text to community and vice versa. What are the most effective and appropriate ways to do this? How will we reflect and discern the will of God for our communities? How will we understand the order of the world and what it means to live faithfully and well? These problems and challenges do not go away from one generation to another.

In attempting to be faithful to the mandate to teach, to bring the text into relationship with the world and our contemporary experience, we share with sages of old the need to create virtual worlds. These are places where we can debate and where we can reflect on the practice of living well, with allegiance to the giver of life. The theological frame that is presupposed by all wisdom writers of the biblical period is an important part of that virtual world, for in such a context we may debate and question without the stigmas and fears often associated with real world problems. As a result, we may be strengthened and prepared to share the same concerns in the midst of a world that may see such a theological frame or rationale for action and behavior as oppressive, naïve, simplistic, and irrelevant.

What We Do Not Share

What has changed? When we look for resources to respond to the mandate for education, for reinterpretation, we look at a world with values that are sometimes antithetical to those found within our religious communities. But perhaps even this phenomenon has its analogies with the biblical period. Certainly the Persian, Hellenistic, Roman, and Babylonian cultures and civilizations were also antagonistic toward—or at best disinterested in—Judaism and Christianity. Yet Jewish and Christian communities incorporated parts of those worlds into what it meant to be Jewish or Christian, what it meant to live and serve God in a foreign land.

Perhaps a clearer and more definite way in which the age of the biblical sage differs from ours has to do with scripture. Scripture is now the community's book, not the sages'. Too often we have left interpretation of the book to priests and other ecclesiastical authorities, to biblical scholars, even to experts in other fields. The reasons for this vary, but one explanation suggests it is a control issue. Who is in charge? Who will tell us how to act? Who will tell us what the particular and special nature of our community is and what that will mean for how we respond to the needs of our present world and the challenges it creates for living in accord with God's will? At other times, it may just be too hard to figure out the answer to these questions, to be involved and immersed in a process of inquiry that seriously questions both past and present. So instead we give the authority and the responsibility to someone else. But the mandate of Deuteronomy and of the New Testament is for all of us. We are all to be involved in the process as both learners and as sage-teachers, relating our problems and our reflections to those of the larger community.

Because the canon of scripture is now the community's book and not the special province of the scribe or sage, the educational process of relating text (old) to community (new) is democratized—it belongs to all of us, whether we like it or not. The search for wisdom has always been for everyone, but the particular interpretive process associated with having an authoritative text in the middle of the community is now central to all community members as well. We must continue to search for effective contexts in which such a process can occur. We must always have a theological frame for this process, though we will be relating and discussing the search for wisdom in a world where many operate without such a frame. If we are to remain faithful to the text and traditions of our community, however, this frame is not optional, for it is the basis of our particularity and our identity.

Several possible contexts and methods may help us continue to be involved in this educational process begun in the biblical period and mandated for all. Taking seriously the methods of the world, in this case using models from art, literature, and music, among others, we might look at practicums, places where we can create virtual worlds and reflect on practice intentionally. Or the preacher might envision the sermon as a place where such reflection can occur, with the congregation involved in such reflection as active listeners. The talkback sessions that sometimes occur after sermons might be particularly valuable if reflection on practice was a primary concern for the preacher. Again, in Sunday school or other forms of education, a practicum could perform a valuable function, with or without the sage or expert. What is needed is a careful look at the community's authoritative traditions and its contemporary experience, and someone who has the skills and courage needed to help relate the two. The time-tried methods of forums and lectures are sometimes very effective ways of bringing sages into the community.

We must be careful here to remember that if dialogue between the text and the community is to happen, we must all be involved. We cannot just leave it to the sages. It is our text. Finally, then, Bible study, always and everywhere (church meetings, homes and families), short or long, builds community, encourages and makes possible education, and is faithful to the mandate to relate text and community.

Conclusions

The problem or the challenge or the mandate of education for the contemporary Christian community of faith involves the world, all of it, and the text, all of it. Moreover, the process involved in education viewed from and informed by a biblical perspective is a fundamental part of our identity as God's people. In searching for wisdom, in addressing the dilemmas that confront us, in teaching, we are called to broad visions of sages. Finally, we are all called to engage in their activities—not as experts, for we need to keep the wisdom of Job 28 in mind here, but rather as members of a community where every member is called by wisdom to discern God's way for us in the world.

How we do this will vary: through being members of a community of inquiry, through practicums, through using and being involved in anything that facilitates dialogue and keeps in mind and action the God we are called to serve. As we look toward this process as a part of our future, we need to remember the biblical sages, to read them, to argue with them, to relate them to our own problems, to bring insights from all parts of the world into dialogue with the text. God, the source of all wisdom, not only is big enough for and not threatened by such a process, but calls us to do this.

This study of the sages and their relationship to contemporary education in our society and the Church is but one example of the text-community dialogue I have spoken of as central to the nature of a scriptural community. Although in some cases it may look like we go to a text first, we never do. Rather, we began with the dilemma of education, or the role of women in the Church, or the problems of secularism, or some other issue. Then we try to put these issues into dialogue with the text. This is, as Ecclesiastes would be happy to tell us, the agenda of Moses and of the biblical sages, of all communities with a scripture, an authoritative text.

We live, like the Israelites to whom Moses spoke, in a new land, filled with new problems and challenges but new blessings as well. We will continue the educational process mandated for our community of faith and reflected by the sages' attempt to deal with the new in light of the old, for the text is a part of who and what we are and must continue to be.

CHAPTER 12

Searching for Wisdom
Recent Biblical Studies and Their Pertinence for Contemporary Ministry

But where shall wisdom be found?
And where is the place of understanding? (Job 28:12)

These questions asked by Job are perennial, as pertinent and as difficult to answer today as they were when first asked. The Old Testament had several answers to these questions, but how helpful are they for contemporary living and ministry? The purpose of this chapter is to identify some of the highlights and major developments in biblical scholarship about wisdom and wisdom literature in the past thirty years. The study of wisdom literature in the Old Testament has many parallels with the study of and search for wisdom in contemporary American society. How can we learn from biblical wisdom and the sages who composed and taught it? The searches for biblical wisdom and what it meant in ancient Israel and for biblical wisdom and what it can mean for contemporary society are part of a larger and never-ending attempt to understand the nature of our world and how to live well within it. While all the answers are not yet given, perhaps biblical scholarship and the wisdom literature it studies can contribute positively to our understanding of both the ancient and contemporary quests reflected in the questions of Job.

This chapter originally appeared in the *Sewanee Theological Review* 37 (1993-94): 151–62, and is used with permission. I have updated the bibliography and provided an overview of more recent developments in wisdom studies. One up-to-date and accessible overview of the last decade's research in wisdom literature can be found in Katherine Dell, *"Get Wisdom, Get Insight": An Introduction to Israel's Wisdom Literature* (Macon, Ga.: Smyth & Helwys, 2000).

Wisdom has often created problems for contemporary biblical scholars. These problems are not simply associated with the difficulty of finding consensus about what wisdom is or where it is to be found. Rather, the search for wisdom, in the biblical books of Proverbs, Job, and Ecclesiastes, as well as in the Apocrypha's Wisdom of Solomon and Ecclesiasticus (to say nothing of other similar literature in the Pseudepigrapha), represents something different from the more traditional literature of the Old Testament, something different from Torah and the Prophets. For biblical scholarship, the question has been not simply what wisdom is, but, having found it, how it is to be related to the orthodoxy of the cult, to the oracles of prophets, and to the law of the priests. Yet that biblical wisdom, with its oft-noted association with institutional power, is firmly entrenched in the life of the world, in the affirmation of the natural order of things, in the processes that seem more often than not to control our lives. This wisdom is not quite so easily dismissed, as some might lead us to believe, as the wisdom of this world, since it is in the Bible and more often than not associated with kings and patriarchs and other seminal figures of our faith.

As biblical scholars search for ways to relate biblical wisdom to the rest of the biblical message, they are mirroring contemporary quests to relate reason and revelation, faith in the God of special revelation with the God of nature and natural theology.[1] All of this is to affirm that to review the history of biblical scholarship devoted to wisdom literature in the past thirty years is to discuss issues of great import to our contemporary world.

To ask *where* wisdom is, is already to have some answers to other questions. That is, we cannot know *where* if we do not know *what* wisdom is, *who* has or might have wisdom, and *how* wisdom is communicated and used. Therefore, this overview of the recent study of biblical wisdom must first ask the questions of *what, who,* and *how* of biblical wisdom and finally return to the question of Job, namely, *where?* A developmental summary of the history of biblical scholarship in wisdom literature and some brief reflections on the significance of this scholarship and wisdom for contemporary ministry follow.

What Is Wisdom?

In 1972, two very different and at first glance contradictory books about Old Testament wisdom appeared. Gerhard von Rad's last great

---

1. See especially the recent work of Leo Perdue, *Wisdom and Creation* (Nashville: Abingdon, 1994).

work, *Wisdom in Israel*, was at once his attempt to fill in some of the blanks he had left concerning this literature in his Old Testament theology and at the same time the fruition of many careful years of study. This work is still generally recognized as the best overall treatment of biblical wisdom in recent scholarship. If a careful and serious treatment of biblical wisdom up to and through the time of Ecclesiasticus is wanted, one can still do no better than von Rad. But juxtaposed to this masterpiece of biblical scholarship is Walter Brueggemann's *In Man We Trust*, a popular volume about the wisdom tradition, which stated, among other things, that a central focus on wisdom literature and its study was really just beginning. Brueggemann challenged contemporary American society and Christian ministry to take wisdom and its social and theological presuppositions seriously.

When looked at together, this rather odd couple of books on biblical wisdom strikes the chords that have characterized the search for wisdom in biblical scholarship up to the present. On the one hand, the field has been stable, yielding few surprises. Our understanding of the character of biblical wisdom has certainly been enhanced by many new studies, but no earth-shattering theories have been proposed that alter our interpretation of wisdom dramatically. On the other hand, as Brueggemann and others had pleaded, we have tried to integrate our understandings of biblical wisdom into the overall biblical message and into our contemporary society. And we have gone beyond von Rad in studying wisdom from the perspective of a host of new methodological and hermeneutical perspectives, from rhetorical criticism to feminist criticism to sociological criticism, and so on.[2]

The overall results of this activity in searching for better definitions of wisdom have, as Qoheleth might have predicted, not yielded anything startlingly new, but rather variations on themes of times past. Theologically, wisdom in ancient Israel is still characterized by a great concern for creation and for order, with many parallels with ancient Near Eastern cultures (especially Egypt and Mesopotamia) still being made. Socially conservative, those who represent mainline wisdom in ancient Israel (e.g., the book of Proverbs) are often associated with the status quo and with hierarchical social systems. Wisdom is intensely moral, sometimes moralistic, and more often than not views the world and its happenings in terms of a retributional system, though scholars will always debate the precise character of such a system, which is shared with many others in the Bible (e.g., the Deuteronomist and

---

2. See Dell, *"Get Wisdom, Get Insight,"* for a good summary of these developments.

lament psalms). Wisdom begins with and honors human experience, rarely speaking of the cult at all until late into the postexilic period (Ecclesiasticus, Wisdom of Solomon). The sages and their wisdom are often seen to be championing a "secular" approach to life's problems,[3] relying upon a reason-based, rather than a revelation-based, system of authority.

Most of this is not particularly new. What is new, however, is the emergence of discussions of wisdom into the mainstream of biblical scholarship. That is what Brueggemann had hoped for, since the wisdom of Israel, with its nonrevelational, nonhistorical, experience-based perspectives, has much to offer contemporary culture. At a time when the fortunes of the mainline churches were waning, when the rhetoric of neo-orthodoxy and the revelation-oriented biblical theology of the 1940s through the 1960s was increasingly ineffectual, the emergence of biblical wisdom as a fresh alternative was heartening indeed.[4] So wisdom became popular, and biblical scholars, with many different agendas, now turned their attention to this literature.

With such popularity came some difficult problems, chief among them reaching a consensus on what wisdom actually was. Von Rad's masterful treatment might have been the logical place to begin, but now that many wanted to see wisdom in many different parts of the Bible, von Rad's definitions were hardly broad enough, nor sensitive to the motivations for searching for wisdom in new places. The study of wisdom and wisdom literature changed from being safe, somewhat detached, even irrelevant to the main currents of biblical faith, to representing a serious hermeneutical option in contemporary dialogue between biblical faith and society. As such, many studies motivated by contemporary concerns (e.g., feminism, rhetorical criticism) appeared.

In the first decade of this fervor, new students of biblical wisdom were primarily interested in pointing out the special characteristics

---

3. We must continue to join the chorus that maintains the inappropriateness of *secular* to describe the sages and their writing. At the same time, we recognize the ease with which this writing can appeal to contemporary readers who do not know or care about the implicit theological underpinning of some (to them) ostensibly secular aphorisms.

4. See Brueggemann's "Uneasy Reflections from a Son of Neoorthodoxy," at the end of *In Man We Trust.* Brueggemann has always been especially attuned to and articulate about the interrelationship between biblical scholarship and contemporary culture. He could see that this new focus on wisdom and its message was but one of many different developments that were, finally, to spell the end of a theological consensus in which he had been nurtured. As it turned out, far more than theology was at issue, for the developments in a period called post-Constantinian, postmodern, and much else have shaken many different foundations of biblical studies.

of the tradition. At a time when the old paradigms of biblical theology were losing their power to persuade, such new developments were greeted with enthusiasm. From the early 1980s to the present day, there has been a greater concern to find ways to relate the wisdom traditions to the rest of the biblical traditions. That is, from a time when the distinctiveness and contrast of wisdom was refreshing and welcomed, we reached a time when wisdom needed to be integrated into a larger and fuller, and inevitably different, picture of biblical faith.

What parallels do we find between these developments and the nature and practice of ministry over the past thirty years? What is wisdom for ministry? Is it to be found in a dominant model (e.g., the therapeutic)? Where is it practiced? How is the wisdom of ministry to be related to the wisdom of the world? Should such questions deal with theological issues or social issues? Has ministry, like the wisdom of Israel, been subjected to studies from many different perspectives, each with its own axe to grind? What, after studies have been done and theories given, constitutes wise ministry, and how, if at all, may this be related to the biblical faith of the sages? For example, could the creation and nature-oriented order of the sages and the wisdom of the world reflected in it be related positively and powerfully to the world of contemporary science? What does ministry with this type of theological perspective and concern look like?[5]

Who Has Wisdom?

If the quest for a definition of wisdom is difficult, it is not because the topic is left unexplored in the Bible, but because there are many different definitions, enigmatic sayings, and multivalent terms associated with what has sometimes been called skill in living. But who wrote the wisdom literature of the Old Testament? On the face of it, we might attribute a great deal of this material to Solomon. But even a quick reading of the books of Proverbs and Ecclesiastes makes it clear that such a possibility is very unlikely. Different stages in the development of the Hebrew language, different collections, different theological assumptions, different literary forms, and a host of other observations demonstrate that this literature has been composed over a fairly long period of time by many authors and collectors. Just as important, wisdom literature puts forward much of its teaching in

---

5. The moving toward an answer to these questions, through a dialogue with some examples of contemporary wisdom and sages, is finally what this volume is about.

the form of timeless truths and, in that sense, it really does not matter who provides the observations and proverbial forms or poems or admonitions that contain this truth. With the exception of Solomon, the officials of King Hezekiah who apparently had something to do with a part of Proverbs (25:1), and a few others in the Bible labeled as wise, biblical wisdom literature does not easily answer the question of who are the sages.[6]

In recent scholarship, such anonymity within the text itself has created a challenge. Who were the sages? What can we say about them on the basis of their teachings? What clues do they give us about their identity? Many different theories have been proposed,[7] ranging from the creation of a lot out of a very little to arguing there was no class of sages at all. But, despite the theories and careful studies, our overall knowledge of those who wrote this literature, or perhaps just collected it, remains vague. Unlike Jeremiah, for example, whose writing and speaking provides much information about the prophet himself, such is not the case for the writers of wisdom.

Still, there are some general observations that can and should be made. For most wisdom, the sage is a head of some sort. A head of family or of state are the two most common examples found in biblical wisdom, though often parent (mother or father) is just as appropriate and explicitly referred to. Sages are also teachers and authors. We would often expect to find sages in close association with power, with the political and social established order of things. Such assumptions have often led scholars to speak of sages or the wise as bureaucrats, middle managers, or counselors to the king. While there are surely loners, such as the wise woman of Tekoa (2 Sam 14), these are the exceptions that prove the rule for some scholars. One other important characteristic often associated with the wise is literacy, the ability to write. This has led some to see a part of the sages' work perhaps tied to the government or the cult, engaged in anything from the writing of treaties to the editing of sacred stories to the writing of psalms. Surely the literary prowess of later sages in the rabbinic period is well known, but by that time roles and functions have changed dramatically and distinctions are made between sages (interpreters) and scribes (copyists).[8]

---

6. The truth of this statement provides another major motivation for this book, which tries to deal with the sages by creating a dialogue with contemporary issues and thinking, in the hopes some light can be shed on these mysterious folk and their import for our times.

7. See John C. Gammie and Leo C. Purdue, eds., *The Sage in Israel and the Ancient Near East* (Winona Lake, Ind.: Eisenbrauns, 1990).

8. See Dell, *"Get Wisdom, Get Insight,"* for an overview of this research.

To ask the question, "Who are the sages in ancient Israel?" is to enter an area of debate and uncertainty. What about contemporary America or the world? Who are the sages today?[9] Do we find them in the Church? Do we find them among the ordained? What functions do they perform? Are sages simply people who know a great deal, or are they people who show us, by their words and actions, how to live well? Does living well have to have an explicitly Christian dimension to it? For many of the sages of ancient Israel, this need to label, authorize, or legitimate wisdom on the basis of association with sacred revelatory and election traditions of Israel was not necessary. What about the twenty-first century? With all the concern to define and embrace things Anglican (or Baptist, or Presbyterian, etc.), do we find sages outside our particular faith communities to be more compelling, more in touch with the world? Why or why not?[10]

How Is Wisdom Communicated?

The primary way in which biblical scholars have answered this question has involved the careful study of the forms of speech used to convey wisdom. At one level, this has produced a great many complex theories about the shape of proverbs, their evolution, and many other wisdom forms we now have in extant literature. To study wisdom from this perspective and with this concern is to be immersed in the nature of poetry, in the analysis of literary forms, in study of rhetoric, and in many other aspects of contemporary literary theory.

Perhaps more significant have been comparative studies in which the proverbial wisdom of other cultures has been contrasted with that of ancient Israel. At the beginning of this century, most comparative work in the biblical field was focused upon the ancient Near East. More recently, however, attention has also been given to Asia, America, and Africa.[11] No doubt this switch in comparative focus has much to say about the concerns and interests of the cultures in which contemporary biblical scholarship takes place. The focus of comparative studies inevitably must look at both the common and the uncommon. While a concern with the common may help to understand the general nature of wisdom in all cultures, it is the uncommon

---

9. See especially chapter 7, pp. 94–100, and chapter 10, pp. 133–36.

10. See chapters 10 and 11 for a discussion of these questions and issues.

11. See Claus Westermann, *Roots of Wisdom* (trans. J. Daryl Charles; Edinburgh: T&T Clark, 1995); and F. W. Golka, *The Leopard's Spots: Biblical and African Wisdom in Proverbs* (Edinburgh: T&T Clark, 1993).

that helps to define the distinctiveness of Israelite wisdom both socially and theologically. The implications of comparative studies of wisdom for our contemporary quests need to be spelled out more fully.
What are we really searching for? How important is the God-language,
which is sometimes found in wisdom and sometimes not? These questions must be answered if we are to relate many of the recent studies
of wisdom to the Church and its ministry today.

Finally, another way in which the issue of how wisdom is to be communicated concerns its presumed educational role and value. How did
wisdom get taught in ancient Israel? Were there pedagogical rules or
special methods associated with wisdom literature and the learning of
it? There are several ways to approach these questions, all of which
take the biblical text as primary evidence in light of scant archaeolog-
ical findings. It may be necessary to go to other sources (e.g., the rabbis, contemporary educational theory) in order to posit ways in which
this literature may have been or can be used in educational contexts.
It is heartening to see biblical scholars and religious educators lift up
the wisdom traditions of ancient Israel as a special resource for contemporary education.[12] All of this bodes well for the future and signals
new and productive directions for research and study.

Where Is Wisdom?

Now we are able to return to Job's question, which is a question asked
by every society at all times. In light of the developments in biblical
scholarship already highlighted, it should be easy to predict the
answers that have been given, both traditional and fairly new and
wide-ranging.

Following the classical approach of someone like Gerhard von Rad,
the *where* of biblical wisdom is located in the family, in the court of
the king, and in the school. Many different distinctions are made
between wisdom teachings found in these settings, with special terminology being employed (e.g., clan wisdom and popular wisdom,
both of which represent wisdom found in a nonroyal setting, each has
its own particular characteristics and concerns). The question of
when and how God gets associated with wisdom in an explicit way
(e.g., in Proverbs 1–9) is continually debated, though there is some
agreement that the sacred-nationalistic traditions of Israel and wisdom do not become fully connected until late in the postexilic period

---

12. See the education section of the bibliography for examples.

by works such as Ecclesiasticus. In either the family or the court, one can see both the socially conservative value of wisdom and the identity of those who would be considered wise (elders, heads of clans, kings, advisors). However, the nature of schools in ancient Israel before Ben Sira continues to be a matter of significant debate. There is little or no textual evidence for the existence of schools. How and where was wisdom taught? Only in the family? Only at the court? The answers to these questions do not as yet provide a basis for consensus in biblical scholarship. Where do we in the twenty-first century look for wisdom? In schools? In Sunday schools? In universities? In prep schools? Elsewhere?[13]

Despite the debates over the provenance of certain wisdom forms and over the precise setting in which such forms are to be found, research in this area of the *where* of wisdom has, at one level, been fairly straightforward over the past twenty years. But with the excitement of wisdom as a theological alternative to revealed religion and with the new attention given to Wisdom as a standard- bearer for feminism and for different epistemologies, it is not surprising that the search for wisdom might expand a bit. Indeed, scholars have found wisdom in one form or another in almost every Old Testament book. And, although this is not the subject matter at hand, such discoveries of wisdom have characterized New Testament studies as well, with new focuses on Jesus as sage and Jesus as teacher becoming more and more common. There are legitimate calls for methodological clarity and restraint in this area. The phenomenon of finding wisdom in many different types of literature represents the desire to understand all of the Old Testament in light of what had earlier been seen as a minority report, a report difficult to relate to the mainstream traditions found in Torah and the Prophets.[14] The historical implications of finding wisdom and its perspectives all over the Old Testament can be banal (i.e., everything is wisdom, which is itself just some type of popular idiom or rhetoric), or they can reflect significant dialogues between those representing different, even competing, social and theological worldviews. In either case, however, the real value of the "wisdom influence" studies of the past twenty years and more is the recognition that it is too simple and finally inaccurate to see wisdom as something unrelated to revelation. The differences we see between

---

13. For some tentative answers to these questions, see chapters 5 and 7 in this volume.

14. See my *Wisdom in the Old Testament Traditions* (Atlanta: John Knox, 1981), and the good contemporary summary of this phenomenon in Dell, "*Get Wisdom, Get Insight.*"

the proverbs of Solomon and the cultic laws of Moses are certainly real, but the bifurcation made between these two ways of thinking and perceiving the world is almost certainly reflective of our contemporary culture and its perspectives, not those of the Old Testament. In this sense, the study of wisdom has pushed us toward an integrating movement in biblical scholarship. To date, as with many other issues, there is no consensus on the basis upon which such integration can and should occur—but the motivation is there. Thus, one way to characterize the view of wisdom since von Rad and Brueggemann is as an increasingly complex phenomenon in ancient Israel, incapable of being separated from other Old Testament traditions as easily as it had been in the past.

A History of Scholarship: From Von Rad and Brueggemann to Clements and Beyond

In 1992, the English scholar R. E. Clements published a significant new study of wisdom entitled *Wisdom and Theology*. Written twenty years after von Rad and Brueggemann, this work may be used as a benchmark to reflect what has been done and what is still to be done, in the search for wisdom. The beginning of Clements's work testifies to the enduring importance of von Rad and of some of the special problems wisdom in the biblical period will have. The issues addressed are familiar: the literary and theological character of wisdom, its relationship to the rest of biblical literature, the special problems associated with its nonrevelational and nonhistorical character. Yes, others have searched for wisdom in different places, others have used new methods and subjected the wisdom of Israel to contemporary ideological perspectives. But when all is said and done, the same problems remain, and we are no closer to integrating wisdom more fully into the mainstream of biblical faith than we were before.

Clements quickly goes beyond such a conception of wisdom, beyond the methodological problems that have prevented others from attempting to see this tradition in full relationship to the rest of the Old Testament. Relying heavily on Victor Turner's notion of liminality and focusing upon the catastrophic events and consequences of the Judean exile, Clements proposes that wisdom provides a worldview that allowed postexilic Israel to pick up the pieces, to construct another society and religious perspective more able to function in its new world. The picture Clements constructs is bold and surely subject to much debate, but its importance for the history of Old

Testament scholarship's study of wisdom remains, even if eventually its main points are qualified or even rejected.

Building upon the insights of von Rad and many other scholars of Old Testament wisdom, Clements has also taken seriously the new enthusiasm over the concept of wisdom, with its secular flavor, its creation and universalistic base, and its particular way of being establishment-oriented in a very nonestablishment time (i.e., the postexilic period). In doing this, he has gone beyond searching for wisdom, beyond discussing methodological problems, and has provided a synthetic and theoretical picture of wisdom fully integrated into postexilic society. This picture presupposes and demands that wisdom be understood and valued in terms of its relationships with all other biblical traditions. Put simply, Clements has provided a constructive approach to the place and value of wisdom in postexilic Israel's history and religious faith. His book suggests that after the breakdown of past theological consensus, after the enthusiasm of seeing biblical wisdom studies on center stage, after much experimentation and seeing wisdom everywhere, it is now time to do some constructive work. Clements tries to relate wisdom to the rest of Israel's life and faith, not simply to see it as the other way to look at and value life.

Many important studies have paved the way for this new emphasis in the study of biblical wisdom: investigations of wisdom's relationship to the cult, the increasing importance of cross- and multidisciplinary approaches to the study of biblical literature in general and wisdom in particular, and attempts to ask how wisdom is to be used and to be taught.

What is happening with biblical wisdom is also happening in all areas of biblical studies. In the 1970s, consensus at a number of different levels fell apart. The giants of biblical scholarship were gone, and so were their synthetic overviews of biblical history, theology, and tradition.[15] In such a context, a new emphasis on wisdom was both natural and welcomed. As the enthusiasm for wisdom gained momentum, it was related to, or rather found in, all parts of the Bible. But methodological good sense finally prevailed, and wisdom became what it had always been—one option among many within the Old Testament. In the 1980s, pluralism was the byword in theological studies, but it was soon recognized that pluralism had been mistaken for the existence of a number of different but essentially unrelated trends and movements

---

15. It has often been observed that also gone was a climate in society and culture that enabled giants, and consensus, to exist.

within biblical scholarship. The matrix upon which all pluralistic realities must exist was simply not defined, or perhaps was not there at all. The work of Clements in wisdom is one indication that work is now being done to help define the matrix, the basis of consensus, the beginning of putting together all the disparate pieces of biblical scholarship, of relating the pieces to the whole once again. Whether this will finally result in grand new social and theological syntheses is certainly not predictable. But wisdom has gone from (1) being a problem, to (2) being an exciting new way of viewing the world and God, to (3) being present in almost every part of the Old Testament, to (4) being finally one very important component in a full and complete picture of the history and theology of Israel. As is most often the case, this development has been mirrored in, and in some cases caused by, similar developments in contemporary society.

Since the early 1990s and the work of Clements, many new insights have been made in wisdom studies. Among these are a number of significant commentaries, comparative studies, theological investigations, explorations of the relationship of wisdom to canon, and research on education, to name but a few. But most of these studies are influenced by the spirit reflected in Clements's work, namely, a desire to integrate and relate, rather than distinguish and polarize.

Wisdom and Ministry in the Early Twenty-first Century

What can we learn from all of this that is applicable and pertinent to the Church in the twenty-first century? First, the wisdom of the world, the values we consider essential for living well and for succeeding in life, is often as apparently tangential and insignificant to the Church as earlier scholarship and faith communities perceived biblical wisdom was to the cultic values and structure of ancient Israel. Those who preach and teach the values of revealed religion in American society must be aware, however, that there are other ways to value oneself and one's place in the world and that some of them are to be found within the Bible itself. Just as important, perhaps, is the observation made by Brueggemann and many others that the wisdom of ancient Israel is compatible with contemporary wisdom, which pervades American society and lifts high success, hierarchical social structures, and order. Putting all of this wisdom into dialogue with the rest of the biblical message is the mandate before the Church and biblical scholarship today. It would be easy to accept the wisdom of the biblical writers, but finally it does not exist by itself. It would be easy to accept the wisdom of contemporary society, for success and status are probably more easily achieved through such a route. But what is called for is an honoring of the value of wisdom in society, both religious wisdom and secular wisdom, for the implication of the biblical witness is that both types of wisdom finally come from God. The trick is in relating the two of them productively and accurately. Biblical scholarship has often studied wisdom and its value with an all-or-nothing approach: Either wisdom is really not very important or it is everything. The truth is probably somewhere in between, and it demands a constructive approach. Through teaching, through preaching (though texts from wisdom literature do not occur with great frequency in most lectionaries), through intentionally looking at the whole of the biblical message, wisdom may indeed continue to be present for us. The question of Job will always remain, but at least it can be an exciting challenge rather than a depressing condemnation.

Searching for wisdom has been an exciting and eventful endeavor in Old Testament scholarship over the past thirty years. In the light of the work of Clements and others, it promises to continue to be as interesting and valuable in the future. There are strong connections between wisdom in ancient Israel and wisdom in our own society. The search for wisdom is difficult, but the rewards are great when wisdom is glimpsed or possessed for even just a moment. I hope that the contemporary Church will join in this search. The witness to the interrelatedness of all creation found in wisdom has much to say to existing conditions and problems in our political and natural world. In such a joint effort, biblical scholarship and the Church will inform and enrich each other while searching for a wisdom at once inaccessible and in the midst of our world.

Conclusion
Searching for Sages in America:
Can the Bible Help?

This study has created an intentional dialogue between the worlds and literatures of ancient sages and a modern time searching for wisdom and filled with those who possess at least some characteristics of the sage. It is now appropriate to assess what has been accomplished, what still needs to be done, and to look briefly at some contemporary wisdom that needs to be related to the ancient sage.

Things Done: Ancient Sages with Contemporary Nuances

This book has been developed on the basis of two special interests: (1) approaching the biblical material from a canonical perspective, and (2) comparing and contrasting the educational interests and pedagogy of the ancient sages with the help of contemporary educational theories and institutions. What light has been shed by these two interests?

A focus on the scriptural character of wisdom literature has highlighted a presupposition made in the introduction, namely, that a sage needs to be related to an authoritative tradition, something ultimately viewed as wisdom, which has normative consequences for the behavior of a particular community. The basis for the norms associated with wisdom can vary, focused sometimes on values and possibilities for self-fulfillment, sometimes on authority and various social systems (family, royal, teacher-student), sometimes on common sense

160

and pragmatic concern for what works. The espoused wisdom of the sage is never far from an institutional reality that cares about, preserves, and transmits the sage's norms and values. This particular focus comes clearly from the normative scriptural nature of the biblical material as it has been given to communities of faith over many generations. The questions such an understanding of sages raise for the contemporary period are: What are the normative value systems and their institutions that undergird the wise today? And how are the values of contemporary sages to be related to the Bible and its scriptural norms?

The second special focus in this study, the educational roles and pedagogical methods of ancient and modern sages, has resulted in a number of interesting comparisons, contrasts, and suggestions. From the biblical perspective, we know very little about teaching and pedagogy in ancient Israel. Most discussions of education in biblical times depend heavily on comparative data from Greece, Egypt, and Mesopotamia, where literary and social parallels with varying degrees of credibility are made.

The use of contemporary educational theories, models, and goals to explain and understand ancient biblical texts and practices may seem to some fanciful and imaginative. On one level this is true, for without some willingness to exercise imagination, to draw parallels between ancient and modern, many of the studies in this volume would not be possible. I hope, however, that some of the parallels and suggestions help us understand characteristics of both biblical sages and their contemporary counterparts a bit better. While it is not necessary to posit that the early sages were "reflective practitioners," or that contemporary professionals are just like biblical sages, nevertheless we may learn from a dialogue between them and a comparison of their roles, values, and respective communities. For example, the use of the concept of a virtual world to understand the function and pedagogical significance of images and poems in the book of Proverbs makes a valuable contribution to our overall interpretation of ancient wisdom literature. Alternatively, the roles of contemporary professionals may be more fully understood by envisioning some of their goals and methods in light of who and what ancient sages were.

What picture of the sage is attained when all of the chapters in this volume are put together? First, the sage is clearly to be associated with confessional communities, that is, with communities that have institutional and cultural norms and values where wisdom is to be searched for, affirmed, and followed. Some sages—Solomon and Confucius are excellent examples—may best be seen as social constructs, larger-than-life figures, whose lives and teachings are somehow inextricably tied to the wisdom of the institutions they represent. The wisdom of these sages transcends what any mere individual could have produced. Similar observations might be made about contemporary professionals.

Such social constructs provide models for both sages, who transmit the wisdom of the past, and for their students. The sages are teachers of values and of ways of living and are found in schools or other settings with pedagogical intentions (e.g., the palace). Sages are those often associated with order and the status quo, with conservative functions of trying to preserve social institutions and the authority systems that uphold and maintain them.

Sages of ancient Israel also have a curious relationship to what today we call the secular. Though the sacred/secular dichotomy is an inappropriate way to understand the culture of biblical Israel, nevertheless, the sage was often involved in thinking and living on the outside of the cult or even the monarchy. As a result, searching for parallels with contemporary sages who are not a part of the religious establishment—indeed, who may not even be a part of the confessional community of faith—is in order. The question of how a confessional community can and will learn from such "outsider" sages is very much at the heart of understanding the implications of dialogue between ancient and modern sages and wisdom.

Finally, many contemporary educators have seen the value of envisioning the modern professional as a reflective practitioner. Such a pedagogical role for the sage is important in understanding biblical as well as modern wisdom. This and other contemporary theories have created many possible relationships and parallels between biblical wisdom and contemporary society worthy of further study.

Things Left Undone: Contemporary Sages with Ancient Nuances

If we were searching for wisdom in America, where would we go to find it? Who would be our sages? What can we learn from biblical wisdom and its sages that will help us identify, evaluate, and use contemporary wisdom? If we begin with a common assumption, that whatever wisdom is and wherever it is found, it enables one to live skillfully and well, then we are met with a great number of wise authors and leaders who wish to sell their wisdom to our contemporary society.

In his book, *What Really Matters: Searching for Wisdom in America,* Tony Schwartz relates a pilgrimage he took to various leaders of self-help movements and of many other popular and important people in America who have been sought after because of the wisdom they seem to possess.[1] Whether it was the study of human potential, or understanding the Enneagram,[2] or eating wisely, or understanding and using meditative techniques from the East, or any number of other practices and techniques, Schwartz was exposed to many different ways to come to a new self-understanding and to fulfill one's potential as a human being in this world. How can one argue with the goals of such movements and individuals? How can one deny there is wisdom here?

Many of the movements and sages who promise wisdom and success in contemporary society use the rhetoric of spirituality, sometimes with explicit religious language, to ground their particular perspectives. The use of spiritual language is appealing to adherents of established religion, even if the sages who use this language are not connected to religious institutions. Phyllis Tickle has written extensively about the phenomenon of God-talk in America, much of which is not particularly associated with traditional churches and other established religious institutions but is aligned with many who are selling wisdom and all of its benefits.[3] To be fair, some of the current wisdom rhetoric is tied to religious traditions, though much of it is not.[4] Tickle believes there are a number of reasons for the new emphasis on spirituality in our society, among them a concern for more morality and for clearer, firmer standards and values. This can and should be related to the phenomenon of the Church's waning in influence and numbers for the past generation in America. In addition, the various ways in which American society has sought to describe itself and its many parts—first hoping for integration through a melting pot metaphor in the 1950s, then speaking out of new voices in the 1960s and 1970s, then describing a pluralistic society in the 1980s and early

---

1. Tony Schwartz, *What Really Matters: Searching for Wisdom in America* (New York: Bantam, 1995).

2 The Enneagram is an ancient non-Western system for understanding personality types. For a fuller discussion, see Schwartz, *What Really Matters*, chapter 10.

3. See, e.g., Phyllis Tickle, *Re-Discovering the Sacred: Spirituality in America* (New York: Crossroad, 1995).

4. See, e.g., Bonnie Menes Kahn et al., *Building Wisdom's House: A Book of Values for Our Time* (Reading, Mass.: Addison-Wesley, 1997).

1990s, and now speaking of diversity—must be related to whatever wisdom is. No wonder, then, with these phenomena affecting our established religions and our society at large, that appeals for wisdom have increasingly been focused on the individual or on the smaller group, promising the ability to come to grips with ourselves, our fears, our sexuality, our minds, our money, our bodies. Eventually, of course, the social matrix upon which we all live must also be a part of our wise living. Very often, however, this is seen not from the perspective of service, of belonging to a group, as much as from the perspective of fulfilling individual potential and purpose.

As we focus on changes and differences from previous times, we should also mention the situation of education. In many contexts, skills are being separated from content, with the former being seen as most important. Such an approach to education would throw much of the classics (literature associated with the liberal arts) out of the contemporary educational curriculum, thus moving even farther away from the *paideia* model of education that has been important for millennia. Ironically, perhaps, our society continues to want people formed and shaped by fundamental values but seems to think this is now possible without immersion in a classical wisdom with sages teaching the classics. And what is the role of modern technology in all of this? Where are the sages here?

Searching for wisdom continues to be an important endeavor in the contemporary period. This search is surely shared with the Bible and its sages. The question before us at the moment is whether or not the biblical sages would authorize the current search, its methods, and its goals. Are all of the searching and all of the books, movies, television, special conferences, and different religions equally valid? Here is where the Bible and its sages may be able to help, or at least offer an opinion. We may imagine a biblical sage looking at what is presently going on in the wisdom industry and making the following observations or suggestions.

"What has happened will happen again, and what has been done will be done again; there is nothing new under the sun" (Eccl 1:9, REB). Surely many of the biblical sages would affirm, with Ecclesiastes, the "been there, done that" character of much of what contemporary wisdom claims. The issues currently being addressed are human issues and have not changed dramatically over the centuries. Yes, aging is difficult and life is tough, but no more so in our times than in the first millennium B.C.E.. That the search for wisdom should be seen as a spiritual quest, as many contemporary writers and speakers have suggested, is a valid point, as long as proper and life-affirming and sustaining behavior is the final concern. What is wisdom? How does one possess it? How is it experienced and made manifest in the world? The diversity that characterizes contemporary claims for wisdom and the answers to these questions would not bother the ancient sages; they would probably encourage us to embrace it all. The nonreligious character of much contemporary wisdom would not bother biblical sages either, for their broad interests could not be taken seriously without inclusion of such perspectives. And the inclusion of Eastern and other nonindigenous traditions and practices into what we call wisdom would surely be applauded by the biblical sages who were only too willing to incorporate Egyptian, Babylonian, Greek, and other sources of wisdom into their normative literature. To the extent that this use of non-biblical wisdom reflects openness to hearing from everyone and recognizing that wisdom is found in all parts of the world and in all its religious and nonreligious traditions, the biblical sages would be affirmative. Finally, when contemporary American wisdom seekers take a hard look at life, its shortcomings, and its inadequacies, the sages would affirm such approaches, seeing them not as new but as critical for the gaining of wisdom.

"The LORD watches over the way of the righteous, but the way of the wicked is doomed" (Ps 1:6). Many of the contemporary wisdom seekers and sellers provide a system, a particular way that, if followed, guarantees prosperity and whatever good is associated with successful living. Again, the ancient sages would affirm the use of such systems, for they too had a system that explained the way life worked and the way in which wisdom could be and should be sought after and found. There is always potential conflict between the huge number of systems constructed, all of which promise success and wisdom. There must be a common matrix to which all the wisdom teachers and preachers are able to relate their truth claims and their behavioral norms. The ancient sages moved in this direction through a nationalistic and scriptural prism. What are the social matrix and common values for contemporary wisdom? How will they be related to the norms and values of the past? Here the relationship of biblical sages to their own societies may provide some helpful and illustrative examples. Surely the goals of such contemporary systems, namely, success and the good life, were also the goals of the ancient sages. And the presupposition that there is an order in this world, one that can be affirmed and even understood (albeit imperfectly and incompletely) from time to time is heartily endorsed by sages both ancient and modern.

"By wisdom the Lord laid the earth's foundations and by under-standing he set the heavens in place; by his knowledge the springs of the deep burst forth and the clouds dropped dew" (Prov 3:19–20). Much of contemporary wisdom focuses on the nonhistorical and the universal, intentionally eschewing the particularity, both historical and confessional in nature, of many established religious institutions and their traditions. While ancient sages sometimes lived within a society and culture that affirmed the particular history and tradi-tions of the Israelite and, later, Jewish cult, sometimes they did not. Moreover, the primary teachings and writings of the wisdom tradi-tion are not historical but are universal in their content and in their appeal. The God of the sages is the God of the universe and of all creation, and only occasionally is discussion of that God related to the particularity of Israel's historical salvific traditions[5]. Overall, then, the sages of Israel would call us to learn from the nonhistori-cal and universal wisdom found in contemporary society, while also calling us to relate this wisdom to the particularity of our own reli-gious traditions.

"A mortal may order his thoughts, but the Lord inspires the words his tongue utters. A mortal's whole conduct may seem right to him, but the Lord weighs up his motives" (Prov 16:1–2). Much of contem-porary wisdom is preoccupied with secular and nonreligious con-cerns and somewhat distanced from the religious establishment and theological thinking. On the one hand, the ancient sages would have no trouble with such a stance and might well encourage us to be open to those whose wisdom has this perspective. On the other hand, sages of old would not be comfortable with a perspective that pro-vides a worldview without God and without some institutional way of speaking of the relationship between God and humanity. The sages might well be open to a pluralism of many different ways of speaking of God. But they would be much less receptive to any wisdom that argued against the need for a theistic worldview. Whether we today must find ways to be open to what sages of old were not is a big and pressing question, especially from the perspective of established reli-gious communities.

If, then, we may find many areas where sages of the biblical period would affirm and welcome the many faces of wisdom of the

---

5. Notice, however, that the personal name for God, *yhwh,* is used in this passage. Thus, a familiarity with traditions that use this name and a particularity associated with this "god" can be assumed for its authors, the sages.

contemporary period and the sages associated with it, there are several places where significant differences occur, points not held in common.

"The LORD created me the first of his works long ago, before all else that he made. . . . Now, sons, listen to me" (Prov 8:22, 32). The ancient sages were involved in a dialogue between old and new, between past and present, and in one sense their work mirrors and models for us the dialogue we wish to have. While it is unfair and inaccurate to say that no proponent of wisdom today seeks to integrate the old into an understanding of the new and what wise action consists of, many do not. While searching for wisdom, many contemporary sages lose a sense of dialogue with the past as a source of authority and direction, becoming so enamored with new possibilities and challenges that little attention is given to the past. This would be unfortunate for us, the biblical sages would say, for without an integration of past into the present and future we will lose orientation and direction, as well as a sense of the source of our wisdom.

"Two are better than one, for their partnership yields this advantage: if one falls, the other can help his companion up again, but woe betide the solitary person who when down has no partner to help him up" (Eccl 4:9–10). The individual is often the focus of contemporary wisdom: how I can achieve self-understanding, how I can relate successfully to the world. Though the teachings of the biblical wisdom writers are often expressed in proverbs aimed at individuals, there is always the presupposition of larger social structures (family, cult, monarchy) to which one belongs and through which success and wisdom will be mediated. The sages are vehicles of larger social structures. They would ask us today to relate the wisdom offered by contemporary society to our communities of faith, wherever they may be found. They would join the critics of individualism in our society, claiming this is not congruent with the gaining and sustaining of wisdom.

A common theme in popular wisdom is achieving and maintaining a balance between the various dimensions and demands of our lives, that is, finding a way to put it all together in a way that does not ignore any of our needs. Stability, wholeness, calmness, and other similar characteristics and goals are usually cited as ideals toward which wisdom leads us. Keeping a balance between the contemplative and rational, between inner work and external behavior, between contemplation and action—all of these and more represent the ways of wisdom in the contemporary world. We are to be integrated human beings, having our act together, clearly knowing of and caring for the whole self and the world in which that self operates.

Most of the people we admire (e.g., athletes and saints) are not particularly balanced people. Yes, we admire the person who seems to be able to get everything done, who eats wisely and exercises and prays and is successful and seems to have time for everything. But such people are often not the phenomenally successful, or the richest, or the ones with messages that motivate us. Sages of old knew this too, and might tell us that the real danger is not imbalance in our lives, that the real goal is not being perfectly balanced and integrated. Rather, remembering the one to whom balance instead of imbalance, calm and integration instead of fierce emotion and separation are offered, and from whom all of this comes, is the goal of the one who would be wise. If that is forgotten, then the rest does not matter. So, balance or not, being on a teeter-totter or not, does not matter as long as we remember who holds it all together and do not fall prey to the temptation that we, or contemporary sages, are responsible for this.

If the biblical sages were with us today, we might witness an interesting debate about the structure of the authority systems that undergird the social realities central for the maintenance and transmission of wisdom. Should we have a hierarchical system of authority? Should we be more collegial and egalitarian? Surely contemporary persons focus upon the latter, citing injustice and oppression of all sorts and conditions when old-fashioned, top-down authority models are used. The sages would raise at least two concerns here. If in our desire to honor each other and to seek equal treatment for all people we lose the rhetoric that points to that which transcends all social systems and that finally authorizes them, then we are in danger of idolatry, making our wisdom and its goals into a god. Societies that have been most shaped by communal values have often been associated with the most repressive and authoritarian and hierarchical social systems. Is it finally the social system and the presence of hierarchy that is the issue, or something else? Ancient sages would ask our contemporary sages to answer such questions with careful attention to the worst, and the best, of the past.

Finally, the focus of many contemporary sages on techniques mastered by individuals that guarantee success in this world would simply not be understood by sages of old. Techniques no more than individuals can be ends in themselves, for they must be related to the larger and corporate purposes of which they are a part. To forget this is to forget a fundamental perspective of wisdom.

So, as we contemplate the many ways in which contemporary and ancient wisdom speaks to us today, who holds the answer? One thing is clear: The search for wisdom remains nonoptional. This is not because the Bible tells us so, or at least not only because it does so. Rather—and here the ancient sages and contemporary sages would agree—the search is built into the structures of the world and into us as human beings. And the object of the search? It is to find the one who gives us life and to be in relationship with that one. To do that type of searching, in ancient Israel or in present times, is to search for wisdom. We must continue that search, enriched and enlivened by the company of both biblical and contemporary seekers.

Looking toward the Future

Where then is wisdom, and where are the sages? This study began with these questions and it must end with them. They are never answered definitively. If there is a direction or a locus for answering such questions, it must be found in the community, in that place where wisdom is identified, however tentatively and however impermanently. It must be found with the sages, who can teach us ways to search for it and who can help us preserve and transmit guidelines for understanding it. This study has maintained that such a community must by definition be a community of faith. It must be a community in which dialogue between the received wisdom of the past and the new wisdom of the present and future occurs. Wisdom leads us along a precarious but exciting path, and to negotiate it well we must be open to the new even as we rely on old ways of understanding that have worked successfully in the past.

Where are we now? What are our next steps? We have identified and argued for a dialogue that is now occurring between ancient and contemporary wisdom. These opinions, both old and new, desperately need to be heard and related to one another rather than used to discredit or reject the old or the new. We need to be a part of all this, for the search for wisdom is a nonoptional part of our lives, whether we do this consciously or not. The search for wisdom and to identify the sages is finally not about which value is correct, the old one or the new one, which way leads to success, the old one or the new one, or which sage is right, the old one or the new one. Rather, wisdom is, and always has been, to be found in the dialogue between the order established in creation and the ever new ways in which that order and life is given to us. To understand this, to live well in such a world, requires that we hear the old and the new, with as many sage opinions as possible.

Select Bibliography

Introductions

Crenshaw, James L. *Old Testament Wisdom: An Introduction.* Atlanta: John Knox, 1981.

Dell, Katherine. *"Get Wisdom, Get Insight": An Introduction to Israel's Wisdom Literature.* Macon, Ga.: Smyth & Helwys, 2000.

Murphy, Roland. *The Tree of Life: An Exploration of Biblical Wisdom Literature.* New York: Doubleday, 1990.

Rad, Gerhard von. *Wisdom in Israel.* Nashville: Abingdon, 1972.

Scott, R. B. Y. *The Way of Wisdom in the Old Testament.* New York: Macmillan, 1971.

Intertestamental Wisdom Literature

Charlesworth, James, ed. *The Old Testament Pseudepigrapha.* 2 vols. Garden City, N.Y.: Doubleday, 1983, 1985.

Collins, John J. *Jewish Wisdom in the Hellenistic Age.* Louisville, Ky.: Westminster John Knox, 1997.

Reese, James M. *The Book of Wisdom, Song of Songs.* Old Testament Message 20. Wilmington, Del.: Michael Glazier, 1983.

Special Studies

Alter, Robert. *The Art of Biblical Poetry.* New York: Basic Books, 1985.

Bergant, Diane. *What Are They Saying about Wisdom Literature?* New York: Paulist Press, 1984.

Brueggemann, Walter. *In Man We Trust: The Neglected Side of Biblical Faith.* Atlanta: John Knox, 1972.

Camp, Claudia. *Wisdom and the Feminine in the Book of Proverbs.* Sheffield, England: Almond Press, 1985.

Clements, R. E. *Wisdom and Theology.* Grand Rapids, Mich.: Eerdmans, 1992.

Fontaine, Carole R. *Traditional Sayings in the Old Testament.* Sheffield, England: Almond Press, 1982.

Golka, F. W. *The Leopard's Spots: Biblical and African Wisdom in Proverbs.* Edinburgh: T&T Clark, 1993.

Heaton, E. W. *The School Tradition in the Old Testament.* Oxford: Oxford University Press, 1994.

Morgan, Donn F. *Wisdom in the Old Testament Traditions.* Atlanta: John Knox, 1981.

Murphy, Roland. *Wisdom Literature: Job, Proverbs, Ruth, Canticles, Ecclesiastes, and Esther.* Forms of Old Testament Literature 13. Grand Rapids, Mich.: Eerdmans, 1981.

Perdue, Leo. *Wisdom and Cult.* Society of Biblical Literature Dissertation Series 30. Missoula, Mont.: Scholars Press, 1977.

————. *Wisdom and Creation.* Nashville: Abingdon, 1994.

Weeks, S. *Early Israelite Wisdom.* Oxford: Oxford University Press, 1994.

Weinfeld, Moshe. *Deuteronomy and the Deuteronomic School.* Oxford: Oxford University Press, 1972.

Westermann, Claus. *Roots of Wisdom.* Translated by J. Daryl Charles. Edinburgh: T&T Clark, 1995.

Whybray, R. N. *The Intellectual Tradition in the Old Testament.* BZAW 135. New York: Walter de Gruyter, 1974.

Sages

Davies, Philip R. *Scribes and Schools: The Canonization of the Hebrew Scriptures.* Library of Ancient Israel. Louisville, Ky.: Westminster John Knox, 1998.

Gammie, John C. and Leo C. Perdue, eds. *The Sage in Israel and the Ancient Near East.* Winona Lake, Ind.: Eisenbrauns, 1990.

Education

Brueggemann, Walter. *The Creative Word.* Philadelphia: Fortress, 1982.

Crenshaw, James. *Education in Ancient Israel: Across the Deadening Silence.* New York: Doubleday, 1998.

Melchert, Charles F. *Wise Teaching: Biblical Wisdom and Educational Ministry.* Harrisburg, Pa.: Trinity Press International, 1998.

Index

Agur, 20
aphoristic literature/speech, 12, 13, 19, 20, 130
Argyris, Chris, 31n.8, 32–33, 70, 72, 90, 93
Asia, 16, 76, 153
    See also China; Hong Kong
authority
    education and, 44, 123
    sages and, 8, 25, 142, 160
    Torah and, 42
    wisdom and, 37, 168
axial development, 4, 11–12, 24, 26

balance, 167–68
behavior
    authority and, 160
    contemporary sages and, 135
    universities and, 59, 62
    wisdom and, 165
    wisdom teachers and, 33–34, 39, 42, 44–45
ben Sira, Jesus
    teaching of, 9, 10–11, 11n, 12–13
    Torah and, 4, 5, 8, 11, 11n, 12–13, 25n.12, 26
    wisdom of, xix

Bible
    community and, 144–46
    contemporary sages vs. sages of, 167
    education and, 30, 33, 57, 62, 119–21, 143–44, 161
    focus on, xxii
    hope in, 47
    sages in time of, 130–31, 132–33
    search for wisdom and, 164, 169
    values and, 161
    wisdom, 29, 45
    See also biblical sages and modern professionals; biblical scholarship; Hebrew Bible; *individual books of Bible*; rabbinic sages, relationship between biblical and; wisdom literature
biblical sages and modern professionals, 84–101
    authority and, 87
    behavioral world building and, 88
    as carriers of value, 89
    differences between, 99–100, 101
    education and, 89
    expertise and, 88

problem setters vs. problem
    solvers, 92
relationship to constituencies
    and society, 86–87
sages as professionals, 90–93
single and double-loop learning
    and, 90–92
See also professionals as sages
biblical scholarship, 147–59
comparative studies, 153–54
history of, 156–58
how wisdom is communicated
    and, 153–54
what wisdom is and, 148–51
where wisdom is and, 154–56
who has wisdom and, 151–53
wisdom and ministry in 21st cen-
    tury and, 158–59
Brueggemann, Walter, 149, 150n.4,
    158
Bush, George W., 53

canon, 99–100
canonical perspective, xviii, 160
cathedrals, as metaphor, 26–28
chaos, 103–4, 110
China
    classroom in South, 80n.33
    Confucius and, 16, 24, 26
    history of education and, 76
    hope and, 52, 53
    parallels between sages of Israel
        and, 47–48
    wisdom in, 21
    See also Asia; Hong Kong
Chincotta, Dino M., 69n.2
Chinese Communist Party, 52
Chronicles, 5
Clements, R. E., 156, 157, 158
Clinton, Bill, 53
community
    Bible and, 144–46
    confessional, 161–62
    Confucius and, 17–18
    education and, 34, 137

scriptural, 41, 42–43, 119–21, 135
Solomon and, 17–18
theses on wisdom and sages and,
    xix–xxi
wisdom and, 169
Confucius, 15–28
    commonalities between Solomon
        and, 21–24
    continued importance of, 24–26
    hope and, 52, 53
    as social construct, 16–18, 21,
        23, 26
control systems, 91n.18
creation
    biblical sages and modern pro-
        fessionals and, 98–99
    biblical scholarship and, 149
    order of, 140
    Proverbs and, 34–40, 45
    wisdom and, 34–40, 41, 45

Daube, David, 7–8
David (King), 18
Deuteronomy, 41–42, 119, 145
dialogue, creating a, xvi–xvii,
    xxiv–xxv
dibbere sopherim, 8
diversity, 164
double-loop learning, 90–92

Ecclesiastes (Qoheleth)
    education and, 118, 146
    hope and, 46
    sages and, 130
    search for wisdom and, 127,
        129, 148, 151, 164, 167
    Solomon and, 19, 20, 105, 109
    See also Qoheleth (Ecclesiastes)
Ecclesiasticus, 5, 148, 155
education, 29–45, 138–46
    agenda, 30, 31
    Bible and, 30, 33, 57, 62, 119–21,
        143–44, 161
    biblical sages and modern
        professionals and, 89

changes in, 164
community and, 34, 137
crisis of, 113–16
focus on, xvii–xviii
future directions for, 43–45
historical framework for, 11
history of, 74–79
as institution, 9–10
interrelationship between
    ancient and contemporary
    educational agendas, 29–30
Israel and, 30, 45, 58, 120, 122,
    155
in 19th-century United States, 60
process of, 10
professional, 32–34
Proverbs and, 29–32, 34–40, 42,
    43, 64, 119, 132–33
rabbis and, 5–7, 9–13
single and double-loop learning
    in, 90–92
sociological and historical con-
    texts of, 45
Torah and, 40–43, 119, 121, 122,
    124, 142–43
wisdom and, 122–24
wisdom literature and, 30, 31, 140
See also education and the
    church; paideia; religious
    educators; teachers; univer-
    sities; Wissenschaft
education and the church, 116–37
biblical mandate for, 119–21
contemporary sages and, 131–32,
    133–34
future of, 124
new roles for sages and, 135–36
religious, 116–19
sages in biblical times and,
    130–31, 132–33
search for wisdom and, 125–29,
    134
wisdom and, 122–24, 129–30
See also religious educators
elders, 130

Enneagram, 163, 163n.2
experience, 97–98
Ezra, 4, 5, 8, 9, 11, 25, 133

Fishbane, Michael, 4, 24
Five Classics, 20
Four Books, 20, 22–23

Gammie, John, 13–14
Genesis, 38, 123
Germany, 60, 89
God
    biblical sages and modern pro-
        fessionals and, 96–97, 100–101
    creation and, 45, 64, 140, 166
    education in the church and, 124
    Israel and, 120
    order and, 123
    Solomon and, 106, 109
    wisdom and, 126, 135
    wisdom poets and, 40
Greece, 76

hakamim, 3, 4, 5, 9, 10–11, 12–13
Hebrew Bible
    education and, 119, 143n.9
    hope and, 46, 47, 48, 50
    Torah in, 41
    wisdom and, xxi
    wisdom teachers and, 45
    See also Bible
hierarchical systems, 95, 149,
    158, 168
Hillel (Rabbi), 7, 9, 10
Hong Kong
    hope and leaders in, 52
    religious educators in, 69–70,
        71, 71n.9, 74, 76, 79, 82
    See also Asia; China
hope, 46–53
    basis of sage's, 51
    contemporary, 52–53
    etymology of, 49
    in Hebrew wisdom literature,
        48–50

In Man We Trust (Brueggemann),
149
institutions
  biblical sages and modern
    professionals and, 92, 93,
    94
  contemporary sages and, 133
  hope and, 47, 51, 52, 53
  leadership and, 102, 103, 105,
    107–8
  professions and, 72, 94
  sage as social construct and,
    17n, 18
  theses on wisdom and sages
    and, xix–xxi
  universities as educational,
    58, 65
  values and, 89, 161
Isaiah, 119
Israel
  biblical and rabbinic sages
    and, 4, 10, 11, 12–13
  China and, 47–48
  Confucius and, 16, 24
  contemporary sages and sages
    of, 134
  defining sages and wisdom and,
    xix, xx
  development of sage in, 9
  education and, 30, 45, 58, 120,
    122, 155
  hakamim of, 3
  identity of, 119–20, 124
  institutions in, 51
  Proverbs and, 19
  search for wisdom and, 153,
    156
  Solomon and, 16, 24
  teaching in, 161
  universities and, 62, 64
  wisdom and, 21, 49, 149, 150,
    156, 157, 158
  wisdom literature and, 46
  wisdom teachers of, 29, 33,
    40–41, 42, 43

Jeremiah, 152
Jesus, 155
Job
  hope in, 46, 49–50, 52
  sages and, 64, 93, 130, 141
  search for wisdom and, 127–28,
    147, 148, 159
  single and double-loop learning
    and, 92
Judaism
  ancient cultures and, 144
  biblical and rabbinic sages and,
    4, 8–9
  Hillel and, 10
  Pharisaic, 6, 9
  rabbinic, 5, 25
  sages of Confucianism and, 25
  Torah and, 25n.12, 43

Kings, 19, 22–23, 105

leadership, 102–10
  approaches to, 102–3
  chaos and, 103–4, 108–10
  new science and, 104, 107, 108
  Solomon and, 104–10
  Wheatley and Solomon, compar-
    isons and contrasts of, 106–10
  Wheatley on, 103–4
Lee, W. O., 69–70, 72n.10, 74, 82
Lemuel, 20

mashal, 9
midrashim, 6, 8, 9
ministry, 151
Mishnah, 5, 6, 8
Moore, G. F., 10
moralistic system, 96, 149

Nehemiah, 5, 24
Newman, John Henry, 59, 63–64,
  67
Ng, T. M., 69–70, 72n.10, 74, 82
Nussbaum, Martha, 60, 63–64,
  65, 67

order
education and, 38–39, 42, 44,
122–23
leadership and, 104, 106, 109
sages and, 98, 140, 142
searching for wisdom and,
149, 158

paideia
focuses of, 59
history of education and, 75,
76–77
Nussbaum and, 60
religious educators and, 78–79,
78–79, 82
sages and, 67, 79–80, 89n.15, 164
Wissenschaft and, 79n.29
Palmer, Parker, 71–72, 78n.27
parables, 9
patriarchal systems, 95
Pharisees, 6, 9, 10
Pirke Abot, 6, 7, 8, 9
pluralism, 120, 121, 157–58, 163–64,
166
poets, 44, 45
professionals, 38, 67
See also biblical sages and
modern professionals;
professions
professionals as sages, 94–100
ahistorical perspective and, 97
canon and, 99–100
conservatism and, 94
creation and, 98–99
experience and, 97–98
hierarchical systems and, 95
moralistic system and, 96
order and, 98
patriarchal systems and, 95
revelation and, 96–97
secularism and, 95–96
status quo orientation and, 94–95
theodicy and, 99
See also biblical sages and modern professionals

professions
crisis in education and, 115–16
definition of professional in,
77n.25
history of, 71–74, 77
institutions and, 72, 94
sages and, 79–83
specialization in, 73
technical rationality and, 78,
78n.26
values and, 95
See also biblical sages and modern professionals; professionals; professionals as sages;
religious educators
Prophets, 48n.7, 48n.8, 119, 121, 155
Proverbs
aphoristic literature of, 19
behavior and, 44–45
biblical sages and modern professionals and, 92
contribution to wisdom literature, 161
creation in, 38, 38–39, 40, 45
education and, 29–32, 34–40, 42,
43, 64, 119, 132–33
hope and, 48, 52
reflective practice and, 33
sages and, 90, 130
search for wisdom and, 126, 129,
148, 151, 152, 154
single and double-loop learning
and, 91
Solomon and, 19, 20, 105
as wisdom literature, 19, 46,
166, 167
Psalms
David (King) and, 18
hope and, 46, 48, 48n.7, 48n.8, 50,
50n.11
wisdom and, 165

Qoheleth (Ecclesiastes), 49, 52, 92,
93, 149
See also Ecclesiastes (Qoheleth)

rabbinic sages, relationship
    between biblical and, 4–14
    explication and analysis of,
        11–13
    roles, teaching and literature in,
        5–11
reflection-in-action, 41–42, 41n.28
reflective practice, 161, 162
relativism, 136
religious educators, 69–83
    in Hong Kong, 69–70, 71, 71n.9,
        74, 76, 79, 82
    paideia and, 78–79
    professional clergy and, 73n.13
    as professionals, 69–71, 72, 73,
        74, 77
    professions and, 78, 79, 79–83
    sages and, 79–83
    sages vs. professionals and, 80
    in South China, 80n.33
    United States and, 71n.9, 74n.14

sages, defining, xviii–xx
Schleirermacher, Friedrich, 77
Schon, Donald
    on educational theories of,
        31n.8
    on professions/professionals,
        32–33, 67, 70, 72, 115
    reflection-in-action process and,
        41, 41n.28
    reflective practitioners and, 40
    on technical rationality, 89n.15
    on testing assumptions, 93
    on theories of action, 90
    on value of theory vs. applica-
        tion, 116
Schwartz, Tony, 163
science, new, 104, 107, 108
scribes, 6, 8, 130
secular, sages as, 95–96, 150,
    150n.3
Shammai (Rabbi), 9
single-loop learning, 90–92

social constructs, sages as, 16–18,
    21–24, 26, 28, 47, 162
Solomon, 15–28
    China and sages such as, 53
    commonalities between
        Confucius and, 21–24
    continued importance of,
        24–26
    Israel and, 47, 51
    leadership and, 65, 104–10
    search for wisdom and, 151, 156
    as social construct, 16–18, 23, 26
    young and old king contrasted
        on leadership, 104–8
Song of Songs, 19n.5, 20
sopher, 6, 8
sopherim, 130
spirituality, 163
Stegner, Wallace, 76n.22
Summers, Lawrence, 129n.1

Tanak, 7, 12, 13
Targumim, 8
teachers
    of ancient Israel, 33
    biblical and rabbinic sages
        and, 12
    institutions and, 51
    mark of a good, 33
    sages as, 9–11, 140–43
    wisdom, 29, 33–34, 39, 40, 42, 43,
        44–45
    See also education; education
        and the church; religious
        educators
techne, 97
technical rationality, 78, 78n.26
techniques, 168–69
theodicy, 99
theories of action, 90
Torah
    creation and, 38
    education and, 40–43, 119, 121,
        122, 124, 142–43

emergence of, 4, 5, 7, 9, 10–13
Judaism and, 25–26, 25n.12
mandate to teach and learn, 143
parallels between educational
    agenda of the wisdom teach-
    ers and, 43
psalms and, 50, 50n.11, 133
search for wisdom and, 155
single and double-loop learning
    and, 91
truth, 66, 67
Turner, Victor, 156

United States
    educational crisis in, 114–15
    education in 19th century, 60
    hope and leadership in, 53
    religious educators and, 71n.9,
        74n.14
    universities, 57–68
        curriculum of, 61–62
        development of, 89n.15
        diversity in, 65
        missions of, 66–67
        models of education in, 59
        Newman on, 59–60, 63–64
        Nussbaum on, 60, 63–64, 65
        relationship of ancient Israel
            sages to modern, 58–61, 66–68
        religion in, 64
        theology in, 62–64
        values and, 59, 62, 63
        wisdom and, 66, 67, 68
        wisdom literature and, 58, 64
        Wissenschaft and, 59, 60, 65,
            67, 76
        See also education
University of Berlin, 77

values
    cathedrals and, 28
    contemporary sages and, 136
    contemporary wisdom and,
        165, 170

education and, 76, 122
leadership and, 103, 105, 109
professions and, 81, 81n.34, 95
Proverbs and, 39, 44
religious communities and
    world, 144, 158
sages as carriers of, 16–17, 161
sages as social construct and,
    25
universities and, 59, 62, 63
Wissenschaft and, 76
Veyrat, Marc, xvn.1
von Rad, Gerhard, 148–49, 150,
    154, 156

*What Really Matters: Searching for
    Wisdom in America*
    (Schwartz), 163
Wheatley, Margaret, 103–4, 106–10
wisdom
    biblical, 29, 45
    communication of, 153–54
    creation and, 34–40, 41, 45
    defining, xviii–xx
    education and, 57, 122–24
    history of biblical, 156–58
    and ministry in 21st century,
        158–59
    monarchial, 19, 20, 21
    poets, 44
    popular, 19, 20, 21
    sages in contemporary world
        and, 129–30, 133–37
    search for, xv–xvi, 125–29
    teachers, 29, 33–34, 39, 40, 42,
        43, 44–45
    universities and, 66, 67, 68
    what is, 148–51
    where is, 154–56
    who has, 151–53
    See also wisdom literature
Wisdom and Theology (Clements),
    156
Wisdom in Israel (von Rad), 149

wisdom literature
  characterization of, 46–47
  education and, 30, 31, 140
  focus on, xxi
  of the Hebrew Bible, 46, 47
  hope and, 47–48, 48n.7,
    48n.8, 51
  portrayal of wisdom, 22
  Song of Songs and, 19n.5
  Torah and, 5
  universities and, 58, 64

See also Confucius; Ecclesiastes
    (Qoheleth); Ecclesiasticus;
    Job; Proverbs; Solomon; wis-
    dom; Wisdom of Solomon
Wisdom of Solomon, 105, 148
Wissenschaft
  history of education and, 76–77,
    78–79
  paideia and, 79n.29
  professions and, 89n.15
  universities and, 59, 60, 65, 67, 76